Triple Impact Coaching
Use-of-Self in the Coaching Process

Bingham House Books
10001 Windstream Drive
Suite 902
Columbia, Maryland 21044
Telephone: 410-997-2829
Fax: 410-997-3381
binghamhousebooks@comcast.net
www.binghamhousebooks.net

Patwell Consulting
175 Olive Street
Victoria, BC
Canada V8S 3H4
Telephone: 250-382-1908
www.patwellconsulting.com

ISBN-13 978-0-9650430-1-4
ISBN-10 0-9650430-1-0

First Edition
November 2006

Second Edition
August 2010

Triple Impact Coaching
Use-of-Self In the Coaching Process

By Beverley Patwell
And Edith Whitfield Seashore

Bingham House Books
Columbia, Maryland
USA
www.binghamhousebooks.com

PATWELL
CONSULTING

www.patwellconsulting.com
Victoria, BC
Canada

Dedicated to the memory of
Dale Seguin (1961-2005)

FOREWORD

TRIPLE IMPACT COACHING

The focus of Triple Impact Coaching is ***Use-of-Self***. It is simple, profound and infinitely complex - all at the same time. Our experience of this phrase over the last two decades has provided us with rich examples of talented individuals in the helping professions developing options where they had felt blocked, reflecting before taking action and checking what is going on inside them before attempting to influence others.

We know the value of instruments and tools of the trade in all of our various professions. We also know that there is a temptation to attribute the success of our work to the technical tools or strategies that we use and the accompanying belief that all we need to do to increase our range of effectiveness is to acquire more of these tools.

The simple theme of this book is to pay the most attention to the person using the tools, meaning oneself, rather than focusing on the design of the tool. An excellent tool in the hands of a struggling professional can do great damage while an imperfect tool in the hands of a true craftsperson can morph into an awesome impact at individual, team and organizational levels.

What is explored in this book is a bit different from the adage, Know Thyself — it asks the practitioner to pay attention to the process by which we make our choices and decisions. It is all about how we choose to perceive the world, how we expand our choices, and then, and only then, decide what to do in the specific situation at hand.

If we listen carefully and inquire deeply, we can begin to see how easily we fall into habits that become automatic and that literally take us away from the process of choosing how to perceive, understand and take action. Habits may simplify our lives, but they also dull our awareness. And it is not long before we literally forget that we are making a choice, but rather think we are simply doing what needs to be done.

Expanding our range of choices and recovering our awareness of the possibilities before us before taking action is the business of *Use-of-Self* in Triple Impact Coaching. Staying open, as stress and the level of demand for action increases, requires each of us to develop support systems and feedback processes so that we are able to deal with sound and current data, to influence in the context of supportive relationships and to continually adapt to the unfolding situation in front of us. With practice, one can develop this action research process so that we are actually in a flow with our work and our interactions with others. That is where the complexity comes into play. It requires us to think in terms of systems dynamics rather than using a simpler cause and effect mental model.

Use-of-Self is a framework for putting theories into practice. Core concepts of Rogers, Maslow, Satir, Jung and many, many other theorists can be put to use if we simply grasp the importance of "on-line" self awareness, reframing what we or others initially may perceive to be important, allowing and encouraging observations from many different vantage points.

These are the tools which allow us to influence the quality of relationships which in turn can facilitate, block or distort our intended outcomes of our work. In this sense, each of us is a theorist about the conditions under which we can draw on the wisdom of those who have contributed to the literature. We can learn much about the conditions under which we are likely to be helpful to others and, on a good day, we can even influence how our clients can use themselves more effectively in their roles as leaders, change agents, facilitators, managers or influential role models and coaches.

Triple Impact Coaching is intended to help you, the reader, further develop your own framework for using yourself creatively and constructively, while coaching your clients to be more effective in their work. Hopefully it will support you in the continual expansion of your understanding and your capacity to be at your best. There is also a possibility that you will find yourself developing your own ideas, theories and concepts about how any individual can continually enhance their own use of themselves for the collective good. In other words, you will become your own scholar-practitioner, adding your own experience to that of others and passing it along to those who also have a passion for reaching their full potential.

Happy reading, experiencing, growing and performing!!

Charles N. Seashore, Ph.D
Fielding Graduate University
Santa Barbara, California
The Lewin Center
Bethel, Maine

PREFACE

As the business world becomes more complex, coaching has evolved into a valuable approach for supporting people through change. Many companies are recognizing coaching as a leadership competency that helps them address the unprecedented challenges involved in building and sustaining high performing teams. More people work in complex reporting structures such as cross functional teams and matrix organizations, in which they have two or more bosses. In these situations training and knowledge transfer is complex, making it difficult to attract and retain the right talent. In addition, people are not retiring as early as expected, so many employers now have the added responsibility of helping their people adjust to career and life transitions.

Many of our client organizations are implementing coaching and mentoring programs to provide support for training and development, knowledge transfer, skill development, and/or as a mechanism to sustain culture change.

The Niagara Institute, a recognized Canadian Leader in the field of Executive Coaching, has seen the demand for Executive Coaching rise dramatically over the last five years. Their clients are using Executive Coaching as a
> ❏ powerful way to develop the Leaders of the future;
> ❏ timely customized approach to support ongoing learning and development which is focused on both individual and organizational needs, goals and objectives;
> ❏ tool of choice for promoting retention and developing effective succession plans;

❏ process which fosters increased resilience, confidence, adaptability and independence; and

❏ process which has a proven track record in helping individuals and teams achieve excellent results within shorter timeframes.

They have also found Executive Coaching to be highly effective for individuals

❏ during transitions into new roles, promotions and expanded accountabilities;

❏ solidifying new teams following mergers and acquisitions;

❏ developing executive presence and effective ways to influence and network to increase buy-in;

❏ rounding out existing skills sets, e.g. development of management and delegation skills for those who have high technical expertise; pulling up from line accountability to senior functional roles; and development of execution skills for those who excel at strategic levels;

❏ promoting retention and proactively managing their career path; and

❏ supporting increased resilience by promoting work life balance and stress management.

In this book we will focus on our Triple Impact Coaching model and technologies that have been successful in helping individuals learn about themselves so they can become effective coaches, mentors, leaders and managers. We will explain our model, provide you with our tools and technologies and share our case studies that illustrate the Triple Impact return on investment (ROI). We hope that our approach will help you help your people develop their coaching competencies. Our approach has also been used to develop successful mentoring programs. We will briefly talk about mentoring in this book to give you a clear understanding of the distinctions between coaching and mentoring so that you can more clearly define your employee development programs.

What is Mentoring?

Mentoring, unlike coaching, is a privileged relationship that usually entails a long-term commitment. Mentors often have influence that far outlasts their own lives. Edie often talks about her mentor, Douglas McGregor, who passed away many years ago. To this day, when she is stuck and needs advice, she often asks herself, "What would Doug do in this situation?"

Mentors may, but do not have to, know the people who look to them for guidance. We can all recall students, employees or clients who surprised us by telling us we were their mentors. Many of our students consider teachers or parents – most of whom probably did not know they were so influential — to have been their first mentors.

Mentoring focuses on developing values, attitudes, and mindsets. Mentors may transfer their wisdom through story telling, by providing examples through their behavior, or by inspiring us to think differently, oftentimes beyond what is happening in the present. In business, mentors may also introduce their employees to contacts or resources that help them achieve their career goals or life aspirations. Mentoring can be a formal or informal relationship.

Definition of Coaching

The focus of Triple Impact Coaching is a cascading or layered approach of coaching from you to your clients, and from your clients to the people they work with, resulting in benefits for the individual, team and organization. The coaching process begins with understanding your own *Use-of-Self* as a coach, leader or change agent in an organization and learning how to be more intentional with your choices to obtain the impact that you need and desire.

Coaching has evolved into a valuable approach for supporting people through change. Many companies are using the Triple Impact Coaching model as a way to develop coaching as a leadership competency within their organization. Our model helps them address unprecedented challenges involved in building and sustaining high performing teams.

This expanded focus helps to support the objectives of the organization, enhances the speed of learning, and ultimately creates the conditions for sustainability of change.

In Chapter 6, we will explain how to design coaching programs in organizations that ensures this connection to the whole.

We believe that everyone in a leadership position coaches other people. Leaders, managers, supervisors and/or functional experts have to know how to help others develop the skills, knowledge and abilities to enhance individual performance, thus enhancing the team's development and productivity and impacting the overall organization's performance.

Coaching is a process that involves goal setting, action planning, measuring and evaluating progress towards a specific outcome or desired impact. The coaching process is usually short in duration and terminates once the goals are achieved.

Coaching is dependent upon the direct relationship between the coach and the client(s) and can take the form of individual, team and organizational coaching or a combination of all three.

We often use Table 1: The Difference Between Coaching and Mentoring to help clients determine whether a coaching or mentoring program best fits their needs.

Table 1: The Difference between Coaching and Mentoring

COACHING	MENTORING
Competence	**Role Model**
Skills, knowledge, abilities	Values, beliefs, attitudes and mindset
Technical or professional focus, e.g., related specifically to role and function	**Political** focus, e.g., introduction to influence networks
Performance-driven, emphasizing goal setting, taking action, monitoring and sustaining performance over time	**Vision-driven**, providing exchange of wisdom, support, learning and guidance to achieve strategic goals
Professional relationship between coach and employee	**Privileged relationship** can be formal or informal
Short-term development	**Long-term** development

We recommend that both coaching and mentoring programs be implemented as learning and development opportunities, not as ways to advance careers through special access to job openings, privileges, or as a vehicle for managing performance. Before embarking on such a journey, we recommend that you understand the type of program you are developing and how it is aligned with the objectives of your organization.

Types of Coaching: Individual, Team and Organizational

There are many types of coaching. Coaching can take place at the individual, team and organizational levels and/or as a combination of the three, producing a Triple Impact.

Triple Impact Coaching, when conducted in the context of a carefully-orchestrated, organization-wide effort, produces higher performance at individual, team and organizational levels. This approach empowers leaders and teams to learn, lead and achieve with greater speed and effectiveness than with traditional one-on-one techniques. Working with individuals to explore their *Use-of-Self* within the context of their work, their relationship with their teams and with their teams in relation to their shared organizational challenges, produce powerful and lasting impact. This approach results in stronger and more effective leadership, teamwork and performance. Through triple impact coaching, many of our clients have experienced faster buy-in, commitment and alignment with organizational objectives, producing quicker, more effective implementation, sustainability of change and ultimately increased organizational performance.

Triple Impact Coaching helps organizations adapt to today's fast-changing environments by building capacity to sustain change through the alignment of its people, processes and culture. At its best, once Triple Impact Coaching unleashes people's potential, it creates momentum, accountability, and generates a critical mass that takes on a life of its own. It is a generative process that re-creates itself with opportunities and synergistic capabilities that were at one time unimaginable, thus reinforcing the power of the collective, a critical element in creating and sustaining culture change.

In the next few pages, we describe each of the three types of coaching and show how they can work synergistically to produce triple impact.

Individual Coaching: Understanding *Use-of-Self*

Beverley recalls a story about her work as a new welfare worker in a highly complex and fast paced environment. "My supervisor informed me on my first day of work that it would take two years of learning and doing to be effective in this new role," Beverley says. "She took her role as supervisor and coach seriously and outlined for me the formal training program, supervision process, performance standards and milestones of achievement."

According to Beverley, her manager was very clear about how she was going to support her in achieving these objectives. Beverley took the formal training program that all welfare workers attended, and her supervisor supplemented this training with real time — and often just-in-time — individual coaching.

"This formal coaching approach focused on my *Use-of-Self* as a welfare worker," she recalls. "We discussed my behavior, choices and actions that influenced my ability to provide client service. My supervisor led by example and from behind the scenes. Her style empowered me to make my own decisions and develop my personal approach to my work. I was always responsible for my actions and the interface with my client. Clients were never aware of her presence, but I knew she was with me, directing, supporting and empowering me to learn how to be an effective welfare worker."

Team Coaching: Coaching Others

Effective leaders coach their teams in much the same way that sport coaches do. Through their coaching efforts, they help team members understand the larger vision and how their individual roles and interdependencies work together to achieve common goals and objectives. Team coaches employ *Use-of-Self* techniques to focus on helping other coaches/leaders understand the impact that their choices and actions have on the team. Team coaching leverages the strengths of team members so they can help themselves and each other achieve desired objectives.

An example of team coaching occurred when Beverley worked with the Product Support Team of a high tech company. This group was a newly formed team resulting from the merger of two functional groups, New Product Introduction and Product Support. The leaders of both groups needed to empower their employees to work better as a team, to make decisions, and help their customers adapt to a new service delivery model focused on self service rather than individualized support. This new model demanded that the technical support people change their focus from fixing the problems to coaching customers to help themselves. The leaders, in other words, needed to learn to coach their team to help themselves and one other.

Accomplishing these objectives required the leaders to work together to break down silos and nurture a cooperative team atmosphere among the formerly-separate groups. Team performance was measured by the shared goals, level of quality, response time and customer satisfaction.

Coaching for the two leaders focused on helping them develop a better understanding of their *Use-of-Self* in providing direction, leadership and coaching to their respective teams to implement the new service delivery model. The leaders participated in leadership assessments such as Myers Briggs Type Inventory, team exercises, a *Use-of-Self* workshop, and coaching conversations which revealed that they had different preferences for communication and teamwork. These differences were pronounced enough to cause conflict and confusion for their teams, negatively impacting performance. One leader was hands-on, detail oriented and wanted all aspects of a project plan documented. The other leader was visionary, intuitive and not particularly fond of structure. They both acknowledged that one was the ying and the other the yang in the relationship.

Quite naturally, each leader was giving directions based on their previously unexamined preferences, which had produced positive results until this most recent assignment where they had to work interdependently. Once they became aware of these differences and understood the impact of their *Use-of-Self* on their coaching styles, they were better able to be intentional about their actions. Working together, they adopted a shared coaching style that was less directive than the ones either had formerly employed, moving to a style that empowered and enabled others to act autonomously and responsibly for the good of the larger group. Both leaders learned to slow down, listen and create space for coaching conversations.

"Deciding to accept coaching was the smartest thing we could have done," reported Dale Seguin, the "visionary" member of this learning partnership. "Coaching helped me understand how my *Use-of-Self* impacted my co-workers and team members. My partner, Daniel Houle, and I had the benefit of learning, reflecting and doing as we were living the experience of leading and managing a significant change within Mitel. Working together, we were able to leverage our strengths to develop the best solution for our team."

According to Dale, he and Daniel struggled at first because they were so different but soon learned to work together to improve communication, create buy-in for the new strategy, and generate the coaching culture they needed to succeed.

"We developed a new race track tool (score card) that proved to be a great success in helping the team and the organization understand the level of customer satisfaction," Dale reported. "It also helped our team members understand the interdependencies of our work and clarified who needed to work together to address the key issues. The race track also enabled people to see the direct impact of their work in supporting the key company objectives. We significantly reduced cycle time and improved customer response time. All in all, our coaching program was a very powerful experience."

In summary, the team coaching resulted in a triple impact. First, the leaders learned about themselves and changed their coaching style to become more effective coaches. Second, they learned how to help their teams be more effective as team members and customer coaches. Third, improvements on the organizational level were realized by increased team synergy and performance, measured by increased customer satisfaction, speed of adoption of the new service delivery model, and improved quality of product and service.

Organizational Coaching: Coaching Others to Coach Others

Use-of-Self in Organizational Coaching focuses on helping leaders become aware of how their beliefs, words, and actions influence the changes they want to make throughout the organization. Oftentimes, helping leaders reflect on their choices and intentions makes all the difference between a failed and successful effort.

Beverley worked with the Director of a training center to affect a successful organizational coaching effort. He invited her to facilitate a group meeting at which he planned to launch his new vision for the organization. Beverley began the planning session that preceded the meeting with the following questions "What will success look like for you and the organization at the end of this group meeting?" "What do you want to accomplish?" "Do you want a dialogue or an announcement?" "What do you think your people are expecting?" "What are your fears, worries and concerns?" "What do you need to be at your best?" "What do others need to be at their best?" These questions helped the Director think about the impact of his *Use-of-Self* and his intended outcome. He quickly understood that he had deliberate choices to make that would have an impact on the expected outcome.

To help him explore his options, Beverley and the director used the *Use-of-Self* concept called reframing. Together they developed a process that he could use to engage his people in dialogue about the vision, helping him "reframe" from his original idea of gathering as a forum where he would tell his team about the new vision. This change in his thinking resulted in a new approach to communicate with his management team and organization. It enabled him to lead a two-day meeting that resulted in 100% support and commitment to the vision and a team action plan.

The Director's guided reflections and coaching in conscious *Use-of-Self* produced a triple impact. He was able to coach his management team (impact 1), who were able to coach their teams to help themselves and each other connect with their role in supporting the larger vision (impact 2). This approach impacted the whole organization (impact 3) by generating support at all levels in a very short time and by creating the momentum and commitment required to implement the action plan.

A common thread uniting all three forms of coaching is the ***Use-of-Self***. The more we know about our ***Use-of-Self*** the better we are at making conscious, deliberate choices that help us achieve our intended outcomes. This is why our clients find the Triple Impact Coaching approach unique and valuable.

In "Chapter 7: Case Studies," we will demonstrate the use of internal and external coaches to support Triple Impact Coaching programs. In the next section, we look closely at the Triple Impact Coaching Model that illustrates our framework and approach.

A Word About Process

Triple Impact Coaching is designed to introduce you to the process that we use to help clients develop their own individual, team or organization-wide programs. We will provide an overview of a coaching program and a development process, as well as exercises, strategies, tools and resources to help you design and implement your own program. It is our hope that you will also use this material to continue to develop yourself as a coach, your teams as coaches and leaders, and your organizational leaders on how to create cultures and mindsets that are devoted to coaching, growth and development. We invite you to use any of the anecdotes that appear in this book as you develop your own programs.

Organization of the Book

Triple Impact Coaching is a practical handbook to help you design and deliver coaching programs with impact. Our book is divided into three Parts that will provide you with context, tools and case studies.

Part 1: Coaching and *Use-of-Self* describes our coaching approach and philosophy. We will explain our definition of ***Use-of-Self*** and provide you with the Triple Impact Coaching Model.

Part 2: Developing the *Use-of-Self* Concepts and Tools. Here you will find practical exercises, anecdotes and examples that you can use in developing your own ***Use-of-Self*** coaching programs and toolkits.

Part 3: Coaching in Action. Aligning and Positioning the ***Use-of-Self*** Coaching Program includes a program development process, tools and techniques to ensure your ***Use-of-Self*** Coaching Program is positioned for success. We will demonstrate how Triple Impact Coaching helps build capacity in organizations and explore how to create the conditions for success and sustainability in your organization. To conclude, we will also provide you with three Case Studies that illustrate how Triple Impact Coaching was used in three different companies. Proceco, a global high tech manufacturing company, used Triple Impact Coaching to support transformational change. VIA Rail, a Canadian passenger rail transportation company, highlights the power of a cross functional team's journey as they worked on customer focus, and Transcontinental Media, a national print organization, shares their experience using Triple Impact Coaching to transform their Human Resources function.

TABLE OF CONTENTS

PART 1
COACHING AND *USE-OF-SELF*

In Part 1, we will share our coaching approach and philosophy. We will explain our definition of *Use-of-Self* and provide you with the Triple Impact Coaching Model and framework.

Chapter 1: Introducing *Use-of-Self* Theory and Application
❑ Triple Impact Coaching Model Overview

Chapter 2: Six *Use-of-Self* Concepts

Chapter 1: Introducing *Use-of-Self* Theory and Application

Triple Impact Coaching is a cascading of coaching from you, the coach, to your clients, and from the clients to their colleagues. Since it begins with you, as the coach, it is essential that you understand your own conscious *Use-of-Self*.

You may find the term Conscious *Use-of-Self* awkward at first. We encourage you to stick with it while you read along. As you become more familiar with the term and its concepts, we are confident that you will find it a useful way to think about how you work and interact with others.

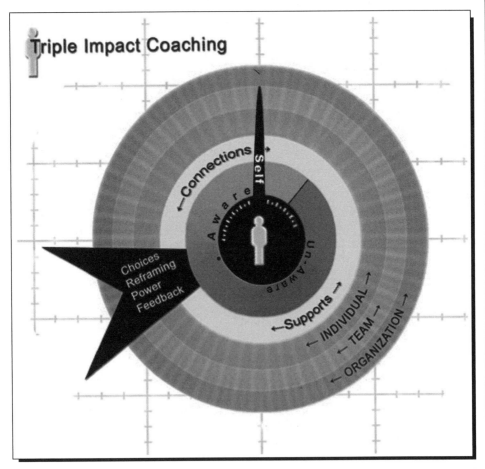

Triple Impact Coaching Model Overview

The graphic we use to describe our Triple Impact Coaching Model resembles a speedometer. Speedometers are instruments that calculate the rate of speed and distance traveled. Most of us use speedometers in our daily lives, in our cars and on our treadmills, relying on them for information that helps us attain, maintain or adjust our speed to achieve our desired performance.

At the core of Triple Impact Coaching is the *Use-of-Self*, the driver or the runner. Coaching begins with developing an awareness of your own Self. It focuses on helping you to move from being unaware to being aware so that you can make informed, intentional, conscious *Use-of-Self* choices that may result in the achievement of your desired performance.

As the graphic indicates, Triple Impact Coaching takes into account your connection to your unique context, situation or circumstance. For instance, in order to coach someone within an organization, it is important to understand an individual's motivation for change, objectives, strengths, learning opportunities, supports, company priorities and team objectives to fully understand their challenges and coaching opportunities.

The speed and effectiveness of your performance can be enhanced with the right supports. Supports come in a variety of shapes and sizes. We help people explore and understand how they use their supports so that they can be confident when taking the steps to effect change and sustain those changes to achieve their desired performance.

The dial on the speedometer in our graphic features the four key technologies: choices, reframing, power and feedback to help you achieve and sustain your desired performance. We will explain each technology in Part 2 and provide exercises to help you and the people you coach.

Triple Impact Coaching is a cascading or layered approach. Working with individuals, teams and the organization enhances the potential for the adoption and retention of the desired changes that can occur at each level. We will illustrate how this works in more detail in Part 3: Coaching In Action.

You might want to consider the following questions as you embark on this coaching journey. What is your desired performance? Where are you starting from? Where do you want and need to be? What do you need to help you accelerate your performance? Are you in overdrive and do you need to slow down? Is your team aligned with your approach? What do you need to do differently as you coach others to adjust their dials? What do you need to know about the organization and it's context to effectively coach others so that you can be aligned to achieve your overall organizational performance?

We will now explain each component of this unique coaching model.

What is *Use-of-Self*?

As we have mentioned, *Use-of-Self* is the core of our coaching model. *Use-of-Self* is all about you, learning about yourself in action. Most of us live our lives with little awareness of how we use ourselves. We do what comes automatically, while focusing on the work and not the impact of our choices or actions. *Use-of-Self* focuses on understanding our beliefs, assumptions, perceptions and actions and how they impact our interactions with others. Awareness of these aspects of ourselves enables us to make better choices about how we interact with others. We believe we have control of the choices we make. We choose to act or not to act. We also choose how we act. *Use-of-Self* is a competency that leads you to be more aware, conscious, and choiceful with your actions and intentions.

What do we mean by Aware and Unaware *Use-of-Self*?

Conscious *Use-of-Self* is intentional and self-aware. When we behave in a way that is routine and reactive we are unaware, on automatic. When we are aware, we are conscious, in tune to what we are doing in the moment. We are consciously aware of information, our behavior and actions as we experience them. As a result, we are better able to make conscious, intentional choices. In both situations we are taking in information from our environment and making choices. When we are unaware, on automatic, the information enters our system and we respond without even thinking about it or our response to it. Being unaware, on automatic, as we react gives us the illusion that we don't have a choice. We often fail to recognize that even on automatic we are the ones making the choices, even if we have chosen to abandon our control of those choices.

Think of how you use yourself when your cell phone rings during the middle of a conversation. Do you immediately answer it without thinking, or do you pay attention to the choices you might have about your response? On automatic, you would answer the phone without thinking. Alternatively, your Conscious *Use-of-Self* may take into account where you were in the conversation, your observations about other people's reactions, your feelings about answering the phone, and ultimately your decision to answer it or not. By consciously considering your choices you are more purposeful with your actions. Why are we so often unaware, on automatic? How did we learn to look outside of ourselves for our reactions and responses? Our learning began early, innocently, as children when we really were not in control of our choices. Adults made most of our choices for us, and we often blamed these adults for our reactions and our responses. As we matured, we began to make our own choices. Consequently, even though as adults we are more than capable of making our own choices, we still revert to the child-like behavior that we are familiar with and give the control of our choices to others. The automatic reflexes and responses built into us by our socialization and our upbringing come so naturally and easily that we are unaware of the possibility of retaining control of our choices. However, knowing that, we revert to old behaviors and patterns. It is possible to become aware of when we do that, either by choice or because we have gone on automatic, and understand that we really do have a choice. Underlying our automatic responses are belief systems that may or may not be outdated and may need to be retrieved and reexamined.

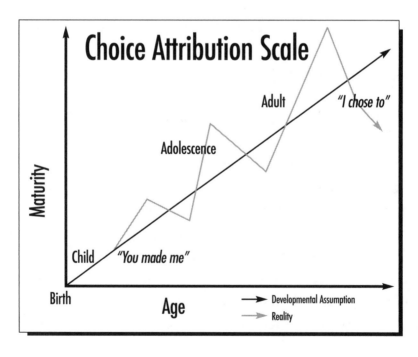

It makes sense that, as a child, we are told to do things by adults and have reactions to these requests, orders, and demands. It also makes sense to blame these adults for their control over our lives. However, as an adult, we can take responsibility for what we do, and have control over our reactions that are available to us, and make choices that were not available to us as children.

It is very difficult to stay in our adult self all the time, so we often go to the child in us, and feel that we don't have a choice and that others are controlling our choices, and then blame the others for the choices they are making for us.

If we are aware when we choose to be in control, accountable, and when we choose to give the control to others, we can understand better when we are coming from our adult self or from our child self. Both are available to us, as choices, but the child self tends to be more automatic.

Moving Toward A Conscious *Use-of-Self*

Conscious *Use-of-Self* is a complex set of behaviors that takes more time and effort than operating on automatic. It is a mindset of continuous learning. It involves discovering, examining and updating our belief systems, being engaged and connected to others. It requires being open to observation, feedback, exploration, action and reflection. We need to keep in touch with what is happening inside and outside of ourselves, slow down the reaction process to permit ourselves to understand our choices, and then monitor ourselves against our intentions and reactions. Working on *Use-of-Self* will seem awkward and time consuming at first, but once it is on your speedometer you will see that it becomes a way of life.

By understanding and consciously, intentionally using ourselves, we will be able to choose our reactions and intentions in the coaching process. The story that begins on page 32, "Knowing when to Step In and Step Out," provides an example of how important conscious *Use-of-Self* can be to the coaching effort. Once we understand ourselves and can consciously choose how we want to react and respond to a given situation, we will be able to coach our clients, employees and others to use themselves more consciously and intentionally.

Conscious *Use-of-Self* is a way of approaching life that leads to increased awareness of one's unique gifts and the capacity to influence others, and to be influenced by others. We believe that Conscious *Use-of-Self* is a necessary competency for people in positions where they are coaching and empowering others to act.

The following Choices Awareness Matrix is a useful tool to help you understand your *Use-of-Self* in making choices.

Choice Awareness Matrix

AWARENESS	CHOICE ATTRIBUTED TO SELF	CHOICE ATTRIBUTED TO OTHERS
AWARE	ACCOUNTABLE	BLAME
UNAWARE	AUTOMATIC	SOCIETAL INHERITANCE

When we are aware that we are in control of our choices, we can be accountable for what we choose. When we are unaware of the choices we have made, we do it automatically by pattern or habit. When we are aware of the choices, but give control of our choices to others, we blame them. When we are unaware of choosing and do something out of our being unaware, we are acting from our belief system and our socialization. We are coming from our societal inheritance.

One of our favorite phrases is that we can't change others, but we can change ourselves in how we react and adapt to other people. This mindset often creates a different dynamic or outcome.

Developing your *Use-of-Self*

We offer three approaches to develop your conscious *Use-of-Self*:
1) Understanding the six Conscious *Use-of-Self* concepts and tools,
2) Practicing with our experiences and reflecting on your experiences, and
3) Engaging others to support you as you learn about your *Use-of-Self*.

We encourage you to use these approaches for yourself, to inform and support your understanding of your own *Use-of-Self* so that you can coach others. We believe it is very important to have a strong support network of people who will help you to become more aware, conscious and choiceful, especially when you go on automatic. Supports can also help you to become more accountable, whenever you resort to choosing to blame others for your reactions. They also help you to become aware of the ways in which you choose to use your energy to give others the control over your emotions, your thinking and your actions rather than making your own choices that could put your energy to work for yourself and others in more productive ways. These approaches can also be used with others so they can incorporate them in such a way that they will be able to help others do the same.

The following story illustrates *Use-of-Self* in Triple Impact Coaching.

Knowing When to Step In and When to Step Out

We were facilitating a team exercise (Broken Squares) in a workshop in which participants were required to complete a puzzle as a team. We know from experience that there will come a moment in this exercise when participants will feel frustrated and blocked. This is often a time of great tension and conflict which can take time to resolve. Although we have facilitated this exercise many times, we still get nervous when we arrive at this juncture, worried that - just this once - our group would not finish the task. Our experience went something like this...

"Don't you think Mary might need a little extra help? Just a push?" Edie asked. "I know we agreed never to interfere with the team when they are doing the exercise, but Mary really looks stumped."

"What's going on, Edie?" Beverley asked. "We've been through this exercise a hundred times and you've never wanted to intervene before. What makes this time different?"

We discussed our choices and the possible impact that our intervening might have on the participant and the team. We explored the possibility that Mary might actually resent Edie's help. We talked about what Edie was feeling and decided to watch a little longer before leaping to intervene. As we observed, we saw that the team appeared to be supporting and empowering Mary, so we decided not to intervene. Once the exercise was completed, there was a huge sigh of relief. People are usually glad to be through that part of our workshop. Everyone feels the tension, although the experience is usually powerful and unique for each participant.

We chose to tell the group about how Edie had made a Conscious *Use-of-Self* decision during the exercise to seek help from Beverley. This choice to share was, in itself, another *Use-of-Self* moment — we could have chosen not to talk about our own reactions.

Edie told the group that when she saw Mary struggling with the exercise, seeming very stuck, she remembered a similar event with another group. "One of the puzzle pieces was missing. It was stuck in an envelope, making it impossible for the group to complete the exercise," Edie recalled. At the end of that session, participants were extremely angry, some felt manipulated or deceived – as they had every right to feel. Edie was fearful of that situation repeating itself.

Edie went on to say that counting the puzzle pieces for the current exercise eased her mind a bit. "I was confident that you had everything you needed to complete the exercise," she explained. "But, I was still struggling – I really wanted to intervene. Bev, however, was able to convince me that intervening would only disempower Mary and may have left some people with a feeling of unfinished business."

Mary told us (and the group) that she was glad we did not intervene because the exercise allowed her to work through a dynamic that has hampered her performance at work and in her personal life. "I need more time than other people seem to need to process information," she said. "This always makes me nervous because I can feel people around me getting impatient. To ease that tension, I tend to give up too easily or withdraw from the situation. But, I did something different today. I did not withdraw, I stuck with the exercise."

By deciding to complete the exercise, Mary learned she can access support and learn from watching others when she is stuck. This experience gave her a new sense of pride and competence that she can now transfer to other experiences. She was aware that, although she had the option to quit, she chose to continue. "I would have felt pretty devastated if you had intervened," she said. "I might have felt that once again I am right to withdraw and let others take over."'

Edie and Bev's conscious *Use-of-Self* helped them make a deliberate choice to ignore their own discomfort for the good of the team. Their choice, it turned out, was the right one – to have followed their inclinations would have been perceived as a mockery of the level of trust and cooperation that the team had achieved, causing them to experience failure, rather than victory. Their decision to share this choice with the group led to a discussion that deepened all participants' understanding of the concepts they were studying. Mary's *Use-of-Self* choice led her to a breakthrough in an area that had been limiting her accomplishments most of her life.

This story illustrates the dilemma that many leaders, managers and coaches face every day. Beverley and Edie needed to understand their own tolerance and comfort level when watching others struggle through a process to complete a task, not much different from when leaders need to delegate, step away and let their teams take over. They also needed to understand how their decisions could potentially impact the success or failure of that struggle. In order to apply *Use-of-Self* principles, Edie needed to be aware of what she was experiencing and willing to stay with the discomfort long enough to understand its cause. Above all, she had to be willing to seek help and support from Beverley. She was able to discuss her anxiety and impatience as well as the possible consequences of intervening. Together, their conversation helped Edie make a Conscious *Use-of-Self* choice. As coaches, we shared our experience with the team which helped them to understand their own patterns of working with others.

This *Use-of-Self* example began with the first level of impact — Edie's *Use-of-Self*. Her choice had an impact on Mary, enabling her to stay with the exercise and feel empowered to succeed. Edie's transparency during the post-exercise debriefing conversation had a second impact on the team. Everyone learned about their Conscious *Use-of-Self* and how it impacted others, as well as how they can transfer this learning to their other life situations.

Chapter 2: Six *Use-of-Self* Concepts

As we have mentioned, we all make choices all the time, even when we hear ourselves saying, "I didn't think I had a choice," we are choosing something. Some of our choices are carefully thought out. Some are automatic. We are aware of many of our choices and of the possibilities from which they were chosen. Our approach to coaching will help you become more aware of the fact that you make choices all the time and you are in complete control of those choices. The impact that others have on you is chosen by you. No one can do anything to you unless you choose to let them.

I can choose to be angry because of your actions but you can't make me angry. Taking conscious control of making a choice means that I am not a victim of your choices. I am not forced to be vulnerable to your choice of action. I don't need to blame you for my actions, my thoughts, or my feelings because I am aware that I choose my response to your actions.

Becoming accountable for our choices — for our *Use-of-Self* — gives us a sense of control over ourselves and instills a feeling of being powerful to do the choosing, consciously, with awareness. We have the ability to see ourselves as continually learning more about our own reactions and the reactions of others to our responses. It may be tempting to take the "easy way out," blaming others for our feelings and our reactions rather than insisting on our own accountability. We hope that you discover that it is more fun and more energizing to be responsible for your own choices and actions. Of course, a willingness to be accountable enables you to be more effective in helping others do the same.

How do we become fully aware of the choices we are making? How do we develop the ability to make conscious choices about how we want to use ourselves in all aspects of our lives? One way is to focus on each of the six components of the *Use-of-Self* — choices, reframing, power, feedback, supports and connections. As we develop competency in the individual components, our overall skill in *Use-of-Self* grows. In Chapter 5, we will discuss each component in detail. The following paragraphs provide some introductory comments.

1. Choices

Having choices means understanding our options and being accountable for our thoughts, feelings, behavior and reactions. Although we always have choices, our power to make conscious decisions depends upon our recognition of the choices. In most situations in which we announce that we have "no choice" for one reason or another, we are unable to see the many options available to us. The more clearly we are able to define our choices, the more conscious, intentional and deliberate we can be in choosing our actions.

Later in this book, we will provide exercises to develop your understanding of:

- ❑ the meaning of making conscious choices;
- ❑ how you can choose consciously;
- ❑ how you can get information about the effect of your choices; and,
- ❑ how you can help others to make conscious choices.

2. Reframing

Reframing in french, is recentrer meaning to be re-centered. This concept helps us to "see" in a different way.

You will learn more about reframing by:

❑ examining your frames;

❑ understanding how you can look at your world and its events through a different frame;

❑ understanding choices and options that are available to you; and

❑ understanding what happens to others when you change your frame.

3. Power

Power is inherent in all of our interactions. Understanding the dynamics of this critical concept will help us recognize that we have the power to make our own choices. We also have influence on how we help others or take away their ability to keep control of their own choices. Agency is one concept that helps us understand power. It requires self-efficacy which is the confidence to act. We either empower or disempower ourselves and others, depending on how we use our agency to help ourselves and others use their power.

Our exercises will help you explore:

❑ how to empower yourself to make your own choices;

❑ how to empower others as you help them to change; and

❑ how to help others believe in themselves and their choices.

4. Feedback

Feedback is an educational tool to help us give people an understanding of the impact of their choices and, therefore, have more control over their actions.

You will explore:

❑ how you can find out about the effect of your choices on others;

❑ what kind of information you need, and how you can get it, so that you can be more aware of your choices; and

❑ how you can, through feedback, help others make more informed choices about their behavior and its impact.

5. Supports

Supports are the networks of people, resources, tools and processes that we use to help us sustain our learning and growth. Effective coaches help people develop their own support networks.

You will explore

❑ techniques to identify your own supports;

❑ how you can create and use a support network;

❑ how you choose the support that you need to make the choices you would like to make; and

❑ how you can help others build their own supports.

6. Connections

Being aware of the connections between ourselves, our relationships within our teams and the internal and external factors influencing our organization helps us to better understand our choices about our *Use-of-Self*.

Our exercises will help you explore

❏ your relevant connections to others, your team and organization;

❏ how you can learn to make choices with an awareness and understanding of these connections and the context within which the choices are being made; and

❏ your level of influence and control in the larger context.

These six concepts, with their exercises, will help you develop your *Use-of-Self* as a conscious, intentional process.

Those of us who are consulting, leading, managing, coaching, teaching, parenting or working to affect the lives of others know it is important to manage our own choices, rather than be managed by them, and to help others to be in control of the choices they are making.

We know this approach will give you the context and the means to take charge of your choices and to understand how to coach and mentor others to become in charge of their choices. We know you will experience these ideas and exercises as liberating, enlightening, and powerful. We hope you will enjoy this experience!

PART 2
DEVELOPING THE *USE-OF-SELF* CONCEPTS AND TOOLS

Here you will find practical exercises, anecdotal stories and examples that you can use in developing your own *Use-of-Self* Coaching Programs.

Chapter 3: Key Elements for Effective Coaching Conversations:
- ❏ Building the Relationship
- ❏ Check Ins
- ❏ Check Outs
- ❏ Safe Enough Space
- ❏ Listening

Chapter 4: Six *Use-of-Self* Concepts, Exercises & Tools:

Concept #1: Choices
- ❏ Appreciative Inquiry Interviews
- ❏ Let Your Fingers Do The Talking Exercise

Concept #2: Reframing
- ❏ Reframing Exercise

Concept #3: Power
- ❏ Volunteer Helper Exercise

Chapter 3: Key Elements for Effective Coaching Conversations

Building the Relationship

Coaching conversations are an essential component of any coaching relationship. The following paragraphs contain a few suggestions to help you build effective coaching conversations.

It is very important to begin building the coaching relationship, either one-on-one or in group settings early in the experience. There are a number of ways to do this by sharing some personal thoughts and feelings with each other and then continuing this process with each session. One way is with a check-in and check-out before and after each session; another way is to set up norms for "safe enough'" space to establish ways of listening effectively to each other.

Exercises

Check-Ins

Whenever people get together in any size gathering, from two to many, we recommend setting a few minutes aside for "checking in" so that they can transition from where they've been to where they are as they enter or leave a session. This process helps the individual and group. It informs others about their concerns, ideas and preoccupations they may bring with them to a session and helps them focus and connect.

Our introduction goes something like this: . . . .
"Before every meeting, or any gathering, most groups find it invaluable

to check in, to let each person share a few thoughts and feelings as we come together." The few times we did not start this way, we have regretted it, because the group had no idea how its members were feeling as they began to work together. The ground rules for the check-in are:

❑ Each person has a few minutes to say how he or she is feeling, to express any thoughts they'd like to share as we come together. Sometimes these thoughts are specifically related to the topic that has brought the group together, so an opening question could be about that topic. Recently we used the following questions as our check in. Give us one headliner that tells us

1) What is your outlandish and highest hope for yourself for this workshop?

2) What is your primary purpose for coming to this coaching workshop?

3) What would you like to say about yourself at the end of this program?

❑ Nobody can interrupt or respond until everyone has checked in. This is not a discussion.

❑ You might want to instruct participants that if they feel like interrupting or making a comment, they should take a deep breath and hold the comment until the end of the check-in. They will have an opportunity to express any thoughts that arise in the course of the check-in after everyone has had their turn. It is important that everyone adhere to the established procedure.

The initial debrief of a check-in usually goes like this, "We'll start with anyone who wants to begin and then that person will call on someone they'd like to hear from." This way people don't start rehearsing what they are going to say because they don't know when they will be called upon. However, it does take a little longer. For quicker check-ins, start with someone and go around the room person-by-person. Or for longer check-ins, invite people to speak up as they wish.

Use-of-Self in the check-in involves noticing what you chose to share. You might also want to reflect about what you didn't choose, how attentive you were to listening, and the reaction you had to others' sharing. Sometimes we start a check-in with the following: "Tell us how you are feeling as we begin the day and if you had any reflections or insights overnight that you think would be helpful for us to know about you as we work together today." The following quote is an example of a memorable check-in.

"Yesterday, when we did the appreciating differences exercise, I learned so much about myself and our team. I did not realize that my diversity played such a strong influence in my work and my life. I am amazed at how after all the years that we have worked together that we share such a strong common value base as a team. This exercise helped me appreciate each person's journey and motivation in their work."

Coaching

During check-ins and check-outs people may connect with what someone said and they may want to continue the conversation after the exercise. We encourage people to follow-up at the end of the check-in or defer until people are in an informal setting. From a coaching perspective, we are often coaching people to develop listening skills.

Many people say in the beginning of check-in and check-out that they find it difficult not to say anything, to hold their thoughts until the end. However, it is our experience that eventually they realize the value in slowing down and listening.

Check-Outs

At the end of the session, it is advantageous to have a check-out. This could be a few words or comments from each person (again not to be joined in or interrupted) so that everyone knows where everyone is as they leave the session. These comments can go quickly in a circle fashion or randomly as each person wishes to speak. Here are a few examples of some check-outs.

"At first, I thought check-ins and check-outs were a waste of time. I now see the value in listening to how people are thinking and feeling at the beginning and end of a coaching session. I learn something about my colleagues each time we check in and out. This is once again a reminder of how we impact each others learning."

"I always knew I was analytical in my decision-making processes. When I participated in the exercise, I was surprised at how I didn't consider the value and input of others. This exercise was powerful in helping me reflect on my behavior and provided me with insight into the choices that I have. I realized that ultimately it is my **Use-of-Self** *that enables me to be more effective in my work and home life."*

Safe Enough Space

Confidentiality is critical in coaching conversations. There are guidelines and principles to help us create the climate and atmosphere of trust that allows effective coaching conversations to take place. However, coaching involves an interaction between others, and in some cases, especially in an organizational setting where there are many participants involved in the coaching context, this can be a challenge. You need to be very clear upfront about what remains between the coach and coachee, what information gets shared with other team members and with those who are supporting the coachee, such as the supervisor and managers, etc. We try to create "safe enough" space, because we have no control over other people and their choices to adhere to the principles and guidelines. In one of Beverley's coaching sessions, her client used the "Cone of Silence" as a way to define what stayed between them in the coaching session, and what fell out of this was to be shared with his manager and human resource support.

It is important to have agreements established between a coach and the person being coached or with participants in a *Use-of-Self* coaching session, so that everyone feels that they are in a safe enough space to share their thoughts and feelings. Those involved share the norms they would like to have established. The following is an example of some norms our clients have suggested.

❑ comment on what is to remain confidential
❑ be sure everyone feels that they are understood
❑ talk without being interrupted
❑ respect individual differences
❑ accept each other's view points
❑ establish a process to give and receive feedback
❑ adhere to principles and ground rules

Listening

Carl Rogers, the eminent non-directive psychologist, said that when someone really feels heard, his/her "eyes will water and a shiver will run up and down his/her spine." There is nothing so satisfying as realizing that you have accurately heard someone or accurately been heard, not just the words but for the meaning that you wanted to convey.

There are a number of ways to work with listening in coaching. One way is to replay what a person has just said, being careful to capture the essence of what they were saying and not responding until the essence has really been heard. It is important to understand what generally gets in the way of listening, such as being stuck in your reaction to what's being said, thinking ahead about your response, going off on a tangent, or tuning out the message.

Too often, conversations continue as if people were really understanding each other, when in actual fact they aren't. It is important to check out our understanding early on.

Chapter 4: Six Use-of-Self Concepts, Exercises and Tools

Concept #1: Choices

Now that you understand the key elements for effective conversations, you are ready to use the exercises and tools designed to develop the six concepts of your Conscious *Use-of-Self*.

We will provide you with the description, exercises, tools and processes for each of the six *Use-of-Self* concepts. Anecdotes from our experience will be used to illustrate how these exercises impacted us, the facilitator, as well as the participants.

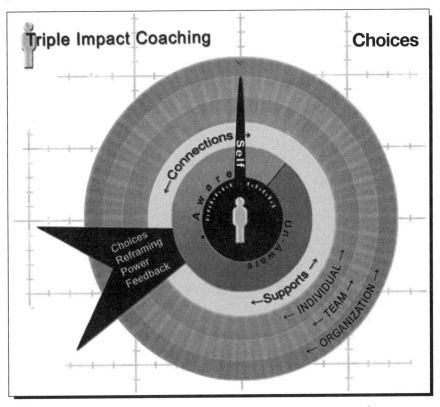

"One's ultimate freedom is the ability to choose one's attitude in any given set of circumstances."

Victor Frankl
Man's Search for Meaning

"At Our Best" Interviews

Exercises

We use this activity at the beginning of a coaching program to help establish coaching goals and objectives. This exercise can be used in a team or one on one coaching context.

Timing	Activity	Responsibilities and Materials
90 min	**Set Up:** Instruct the group to get into pairs. **Process:** Each member of the pair will have a turn to be the interviewer and the interviewee. Each interview should last about 5 minutes. The role of the interviewer, while the person is recalling their story, is to help them to get back in touch and relive their experience. Their job is to ask questions to help the interviewee explore how they were feeling when they were at their very best. Who else was there? What did they actually do? What conditions existed for them to be at their best? It is not necessary to capture all the specifics but to focus on the essence of the experience. After 5-6 minutes, the roles will be reversed and the previous interviewer will become the interviewee. The interviewee will become the interviewer. **Task:** You are asked to recall a time when you were at your best as a coach or being coached. It can be a work situation or life situation. Your example can be recent or in the past. After your interviews you will be asked to present to the group the essence of when your interviewee is at his or her best.	

Timing	Activity	Responsibilities and Materials
	You will tell the story using the first person voice, as though you are your interviewee. For example, if Beverley and Edie were doing this exercise in a pair, after interviewing each other, Beverley would tell the essence of Edie's story beginning with "Hello I am Edie. The time I was at my best as a coach was...." And then Edie would tell Beverley's story in the same manner. **Story Telling:** Facilitators may have to correct people in the beginning as it might be difficult for some people to use the "I" language. **Debrief:** *Use-of-Self:* What did you discover about yourself when you were using yourself at your very best? How would you describe the behaviors in general that one uses when they are being coached or coaching at their very best? **Listening Skills:** What did you realize about your ability to listen in order to retain the essence of someone's story? What were some of the ways you realized you were diverting yourself from listening? **General Observations about Coaching:** What were some of the themes and patterns that you noticed about what is happening for people when their ***Use-of-Self*** is at their very best? What is happening to people when they are coaching others to be at their very best? **Belief Systems:** What did you discover about your ***Use-of-Self*** at your best? What were your beliefs about sharing yourself at your very best? How did you feel hearing someone else tell your story? What belief systems were beneath those feelings?	

Rule of Thumb:

After everyone has had their interviews and brought together the themes of coaching and *Use-of-Self* at one's very best, we talk about how important it is to have our stories available to us, especially when we are not feeling that we are doing well or when we are anxious or concerned about ourselves and how we are behaving. It is at these times, recalling how we felt at our very best, that helps us feel good about ourselves and remember that we can replicate these stories and feelings in our present coaching situations.

This is an entertaining twist because it lets each person hear someone else tell his/her story and it also focuses on the necessity to fully listen in order to be able to share the essence of another person's story. In other words, to really fully understand what it is like to walk in another person's shoes.

This activity always brings a very positive, upbeat mood to the group and it also recalls for the participants how they could recapture some of the behaviors and feelings they had when they were making the very best use of themselves.

Exercises

Let Your Fingers Do The Talking Exercise

On the following page is an exercise that highlights our control over our choices.

Timing	Activity	Responsibilities and Materials
5 min	**Let your fingers do the walking exercise** **Setting the context** This exercise is very experiential and works very well in training or coaching sessions.	Facilitator Coach/Observer Groups of 4 or 5 participants
Rule of Thumb	Objective: To create a situation that brings people out of their comfort zone and is unusual enough to help them gain awareness and understanding of their behavior with others and their belief systems. Although the activity itself takes only 5 minutes, it may take much longer for participants to finish discussing what they have learned during the debriefing segment of the exercise. Lifetime patterns show up very quickly and can be observed and talked about. Optional: You may want to ask an observer to sit outside the group to provide feedback following the exercise. If you do not have enough people for this role, the facilitator can walk around the room and provide feedback in the debrief portion of the exercise.	
5 min.	**Instructions:** Observers are silent during this exercise This exercise will last 5 min. 1. Instruct participants to sit on the floor in a circle as if they are going to play cards. 2. Remove all objects from the space inside the circle, including legs, arms, etc. 3. All participants identify a small space in front of them as their private place. They can return to that space when they don't want to be part of the meeting. 4. Ask everyone to choose a hand to send to the meeting and make sure that the other hand is unavailable. 5. Then say, "We are going to have a 5 min. meeting in silence. You can only use the hand you selected to participate in the meeting."	Facilitator

Timing	Activity	Responsibilities and Materials
	6. The meeting topics and activities are of your group's choice. 7. Participants are not allowed to speak. Use your "go-to-meeting" hand to communicate. 8. The floor space and the air space in the middle of the group is available for their use. 9. The facilitator will call off each minute as it goes by (4, 3, 2, 1, 15 sec.) 10. Ask if anyone has a question before beginning. 11. Begin the 5 min. meeting. 12. Call out when the meeting is over	
15 to 20 min.	**Debrief & Relief** Because this exercise is designed to take people out of their comfort zones, you will often see and hear signs of relief that it is over. Many times, people think the exercise was longer than 5 min. We recommend you debrief the exercise along the lines of your objectives and purpose for choosing this exercise. Example: To better understand non-verbal communication, we debriefed the exercise by exploring the participants' ability to communicate, what they focused on, the choices each person made to communicate or not, the impact of touch, confusion, etc. If you chose to use observers, you might start the debrief by asking them to provide feedback to their small group. Then you can debrief the larger group's experience. Here is the debrief process we often use with our clients. In their small groups, participants spend a few minutes talking to each other about their experience. They may explore the questions presented on the next page:	Facilitators and Coaches

Timing	Activity	Responsibilities and Materials
	Communications: Were you successful in your communication? Did other team members understand your message(s)? What did you do? What did you try to do? What did you think you did? How were your actions and behavior interpreted and experienced by others? *Use-of-Self:* How did you think you were using your Self? Was this familiar behavior or did it surprise you? What feedback can other members give you? Spend a few minutes giving each other feedback on *Use-of-Self*. **Choice of hand:** How deliberate was your choice of hand that you used? Were you aware of your choice? Why did you choose the one you used? What impact did this choice have on your experience? **Belief Systems:** What was your belief system as you entered the exercise? Did you believe you could learn something new or try out new behavior? Did you block yourself? Is this typical of your approach in situations that are new, different or unusual for you? Did you allow yourself to fully participate in this experience? If you were skeptical or believed that this was going to be useless, how did it impact your participation? If you believed it would be interesting and/or challenging, how did it impact you?	

Timing	Activity	Responsibilities and Materials
	In addition to these topics, you might want to explore other possible themes that may surface in the groups: Homogeneous gender groups (male only, female only) vs. mixed gender Expressive with affection vs. task focused Communication: How clearly did people get their points across?	
	Rule of Thumb While the groups are working, we walk around and keep an eye on what is going on. We watch to make sure no one is talking or using their other hand. We try to keep them working with the hand they selected. This exercise is unusual enough (non-verbal) so that people get an insight into their behavior that they don't see in their usual meetings. People can learn how clear they are in their communications by exploring their intentions and any misunderstandings about how they express their intentions. People often think they are clear when they are not and can get frustrated.What did you choose to do? What did you choose not to do rather that giving others responsibility for your behaviors?	
5 min.	**Wrap Up** Acknowledge that this excursion out of the comfort zone may have been difficult for some participants. This was purposeful, chosen to provide an opportunity for learning. We believe that we will only begin to learn about ourselves in a different way when we are behaving differently and often times out of our comfort zone. Instruct the group to write or capture any insights they may have gotten from this exercise.	

Rule of Thumb

You might see a wide range of reactions: people being creative, innovative, playful, uncomfortable, disbelief, and/or skeptical.

Generally participants fall into a routine or pattern as soon as they decide to participate fully. They may be sensual, quiet, reflective, or thoughtful. A group may appear stuck because members are reluctant to try out new behaviors. People often report that they recognize familiar or typical behavior of themselves and their teammates. Those who try out new behavior are surprised by the reactions of others.

Example: Giving Yourself Permission

A woman in one group appeared to be going along with the group UNTIL she flipped the bird (gave the finger). This was out of character for her and she surprised herself and shocked the group. She was a minister's wife and daughter, always a good little girl, and this behavior wasn't very proper. She deliberately chose to use her least dominant hand for this exercise because she wanted to see what would happen— it was the other hand that behaved in this surprising manner. She said she realized her unexpected behavior expressed a secret urge to break out of the mold in which she had confined herself. She was very excited and energized by the experience.

So this exercise can help people identify behaviors and beliefs and give themselves permission to change them. It can also create a better understanding of how people implement their *Use-of-Self* by helping them explore a part of themselves that they may not be expressing.

Appreciating Differences - Vivre La Difference Exercise

Relationships, teams, and organizations can be greatly enhanced by increasing the diversity among the members and genuinely appreciating and leveraging this diversity. We have an exercise that helps participants look at the differences and similarities among them. In addition, this exercise illustrates how important it is to get to know more about the people you coach and work with, so you can have a better understanding of how to be helpful to them.

Exercises

Timing	Activity	Responsibilities and Materials
90 min	**Objective:** To provide an opportunity for people to learn about their diversity and how it impacts their relationships, and to understand the similarities within the team or group. **Room Set up:** Arrange the room in a circle of chairs	Paper and pencil
5 min	Instruct participants to spend a moment by themselves thinking about their answers to the following questions that they will be asked to share with the group. 1. Where were you born and brought up? ❑ What impact did this have on you? 2. Where were your ancestors from? ❑ What impact did this have on you? 3. What was your family life like? ❑ What impact did this have on you? 4. When did you first realize that you were different, unique or special in a significant way? ❑ What was the impact on you then and now? 5. What were some significant events in your life? ❑ What impact did they have on you?	

Timing	Activity	Responsibilities and Materials
60 min	**Story Telling** **Ground rules:** Before you begin sharing the stories, tell participants that there will be no dialogue during the exercise. Every person will have 5-10 minutes to tell his/her story. After each person is finished speaking you can ask a few questions for clarification or understanding.	
25 min	**Debrief:** How did you feel during the exercise? How did you feel when you told your story? How did you feel hearing other people tell their story? What did you notice in terms of similarities? Themes? Patterns? Did you discover anything about yourself that surprised you? Are there opportunities to leverage the diversity in the team so we can be more effective?	

This exercise is very powerful for most of the participants. It informs them of what they chose to share and what they chose not to share. They discover whether or not they were choiceful or automatic. They also discover a lot about the group and are generally amazed at how much closer they feel to each other because of their sharing. It is a powerful experience.

Rule of Thumb

This might look simple but it brings out very deep insights and conversations. Some people may be surprised by the emotion that comes up when they share their life experiences. For others it might not be so obvious. They may be emotional because something they heard from another person's story triggered something in them. Some people may be surprised with the level of transparency, openness and actual content that is shared. You need to scan your group and may need to follow up with people depending on their reactions.

Reflections

Questions for Reflection

> ❑ How does your *Use-of-Self* affect your choices?
> ❑ When do you make conscious deliberate choices?
> ❑ What gets in your way?

Resources

Additional Resources

Emotional Intelligence by Daniel Goleman (1995)
Theory of how emotions and self-awareness play in intelligence.

FIRO B and MBTI Assessment Tools through Consulting Psychologists Press, Inc. (CPP)
www.cpp-db.com (USA) and www.psychometrics.com (Canada).

These tools are useful in helping people to understand and appreciate their own preferences and the diversity of styles that other people may use. This knowledge helps them learn about different choices for their own behavior so that they can adapt to a variety of styles and situations.

Both tools are available online, in hard copy and multiple languages. They are also available in report format to help people develop learning plans.

Myers Briggs Type Inventory (MBTI):
A very useful tool to help people understand their preferences on the following dimensions: extraversion and introversion, sensing and intuition, thinking and feeling and perceiving and judging. MBTI is used to help people in their personal and professional lives. It also helps people understand workplace preferences, how to manage stress, reduce conflict, manage career transitions and improve team performance.

Fundamental Interpersonal Relations Orientation-Behavior (FIRO B):
An assessment tool that is very useful in understanding group and individual development through the stages of inclusion, control and affection.

Concept #2: Reframing

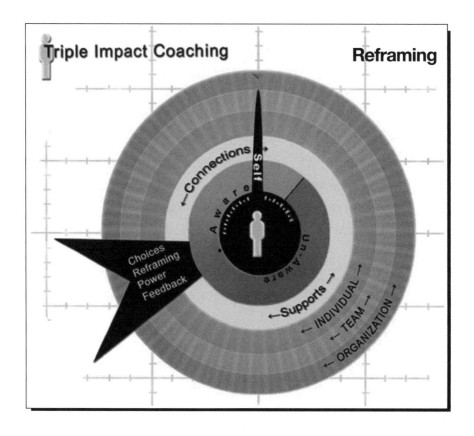

"If you change the way you look at things, the things you look at will change."

Wayne Dyer
Author and Motivational Speaker

Reframing is about changing the meaning we attach to an experience, person or context so that we can understand ourselves and how we may be blocking, influencing or impacting a given situation. Seeing something from a different perspective or angle gives us an opportunity to change the meaning we give it, and may result in more intentional and conscious choices and actions.

Before we can reframe, we must understand our frames, values, beliefs, meanings and perceptions. Our frames come from our inheritance, or belief system, and continue to shape our behavior in positive and negative ways.

Knowing our own frames (and how we see the world through them), helps us to better understand when and how we can reframe in a given situation. Reframing helps us view a problem, situation or conflict from a different perspective or angle, and to look at the impossible and make it possible. If we need a way to see the world differently, we can stop ourselves with the phrase, "Up until now," and then try to reshape the frame to bring us up-to-date. For example: If someone says, "I never thought I could do it." You can say, "up until now"… and watch the confidence rise.

Reframing

❏ gives us control;

❏ helps us to see more objectively;

❏ reduces emotionality;

❏ creates more choices, strategies for creating win-win situations; and,

❏ produces more conscious results.

Edie tells this Rainy Day tale:

One day when my daughter, Becky, was four years old we were supposed to do a number of activities around town. It was pouring rain that day and I said to Becky, "We can't do what we planned to do today because it is a lousy, crummy, miserable day outside." Becky looked at me, looked outside, and then said, "No Mommy, it's a rainy day." I looked again, and through her frame it was a rainy day, and that's all. So, we went out into the rain and had a great time. Where did my frame of a lousy, crummy, miserable day come from? I remember hearing that phrase early and often in my childhood. The memories I recalled were, "if you went outside in the rain, you'd get wet, then you'd get pneumonia and you'd die." A frame that I still put around rainy days, even though over the years I had to have been in the rain, surely gotten wet, never had pneumonia, and am here to tell the tale. However, to this day, my first thoughts on a rainy day are my old frame, and then quickly and consciously I go to my reframe and am off and running.

Old frames are part of our automatic conditioning and can be changed. Here is an exercise to help you practice reframing.

Exercises

Reframing Exercise

Timing	Activity	Responsibilities and Materials
	Step 1: Form pairs who will work together for 60 minutes.	paper, pencil, flip chart
5 min	**Step 2: Select Characteristics (adverbs or adjectives)** Instruct participants to draw three columns on a piece of paper. Demonstrate this for the group. Instruct participants to write four to five characteristics (adverbs or adjectives) that they value about themselves. In column 1. Edie's example: "I always put down two of my own— energetic and smart."	This part is done individually and silently.

Characteristics about myself that I value		
smart		
energetic		

Timing	Activity	Responsibilities and Materials
5 min x 2	**Step 3: Share your characteristics with your partner.** Each pair then shares their characteristics with each other. Ask them to also talk about why they value these characteristics.	Pairs
5 min	**Step 4: Select some Characteristics for group example** When everyone has had an opportunity to share their characteristics, ask 5 or 6 participants to call out one characteristic from their column 1. Record those characteristics in column 1 on the flip chart.	Large Group
5 min	**Step 5: Complete Psychological Opposite column** The second column is called the Psychological Opposite. Working from the same flip chart, write a psychological opposite for each of the characteristics in the first column. These opposites can not include words that begin with "non," "un," "dis," unless they are different words than the ones listed in the characteristics column. For instance, if my characteristic is energetic, then my psychological opposite might be lazy, not non-energetic. If my characteristic is honest, the psychological opposite could be deceptive, but not dishonest. The goal is to get people to thinking more deeply about the individual values they bring to certain words. Using prefixes does not contribute to that goal. | Characteristics about myself that I value	Psychological Opposite	| |---|---|---|
smart	dumb	
energetic	lazy			Individually

Timing	Activity	Responsibilities and Materials
5 min x 2	**Step 6: Share results in pairs** Instruct participants to share their own psychological opposites and what they mean to them. If they need assistance to get a psychological opposite, their partners can help.	Pairs
5 min	**Step 7: Share Psychological Opposites for words on chart.** Using the same flip chart, complete the Psychological Opposite column on the flip chart. Ask each individual who contributed characteristics to column 1 to share what they chose as their psychological opposite for that characteristic. Write those opposites in column 2. This part of the exercise may bring out a variety of reactions. People may not like talking about or describing their psychological opposite. Some people try to influence or soften the description for others. Try to encourage people to be honest about their description. For example, if someone selects honest as their psychological opposite, others might respond with other descriptors that they think are more appropriate. Check with the persons who shared their psychological opposites with the larger group to make sure they consider the description is accurate for them. Each one of us would have a different psychological opposite to our own valued characteristics. After everyone has shared psychological opposites, ask how they feel when they are acting as their psychological opposite. Even if we can't tolerate our psychological opposite, we sometimes act that way. Generally, people respond that they don't feel good about themselves when they are acting out their psychological opposite. Our psychological opposites are parts of our behaviour that we don't like about ourselves. Since we find them unacceptable behavior in ourselves, we are likely to have difficulty accepting these behaviors in others. These behaviors prompt us to get into conflict, dismiss and even dislike others. That leads to column 3.	Flip chart Facilitator Large Group

Timing	Activity	Responsibilities and Materials
5 min x 2	**Step 8: Complete the Reframe column.** Following the approach used to complete columns 1 and 2, instruct participants to individually think of a reframe for each of their psychological opposites. The reframe should be an adjective or adverb that would make the behavior acceptable to oneself and makes it easier for them to work with others who demonstrate that behavior. To help develop the reframe, it is often helpful to consider how you feel when you act in your psychological opposite, which may be similar to how others feel when they act in ways that you find not acceptable. An example of these reframes could be as follows:	Facilitator
5min x 2	**Step 9: Complete Reframe column** In same pairs, participants complete the reframe column.	Pairs
5 min	**Step 10: Call out Reframes** Complete column 3 in the larger group, finding acceptable alternatives to the words already on the flip chart in columns 1 and 2. Check with all participants to determine if their reframe helps them accept their psychological opposite in themselves and others.	Large Group
5 min	**Step 11: Discuss implications for their *Use-of-Self*** When we do this exercise we are often asked, "Are we fooling ourselves?" "Does this really work?" Our experience is that reframing really works when the reframed behavior is really acceptable to the person who is doing the reframing.	Large Group

In Step 8:

Characteristics about myself that I value	Psychological Opposite	Reframe
smart	dumb	naive
energetic	lazy	cooling it or vegging out

Example: Dumb - Naïve, Lazy - Vegging Out

Edie often shares the following two stories of reframing, dumb and lazy, to illustrate the impact of reframing.

> What does dumb - the psychological opposite of smart
> - mean to me? I can still hear my father saying to me
> when I was a child, "That was dumb, use your head," or
> "That was a dumb question to ask," etc. Now, as an adult,
> consultant and teacher, can you imagine how effective I
> would be if I said to a student, "That was really a dumb
> question. Does anyone have a smart question?"
> However, in reframing dumb to naïve (which for me
> means simply "not knowing"), I can accept myself as not
> being dumb, but rather, as not knowing yet and I can
> accept that characteristic more readily in others. This
> has been a very worthwhile reframe for me.

> It was, likewise, impossible for me to find lazy an
> acceptable characteristic, because it was so
> unacceptable in my family when I was growing up. As
> an adult it is difficult for me not to be doing something
> meaningful, to be working on something. Even
> vacations are unacceptable to me.

> This aversion to leisure was pointed out years ago by
> my then 10-year-old daughter as she watched me in the
> kitchen one evening. She said, "Why don't you come
> home like other mothers and get into some jeans and
> relax?" I answered, as I happily peeled potatoes, "I am
> relaxed. Why do you say that?" And she said, "But you still
> have your purse hanging on your shoulder." And so I did.

My daughter helped me find an acceptable reframe for lazy. She came home from school one afternoon and settled in to watch an hour of TV before helping me clean the garage. When I pointed this out, she said, "I'll be with you shortly. I'm vegging out." Vegging out immediately struck me as more appealing than lazy, as did another of her reframes, "cooling it." These two reframes have made the characteristic "lazy" much more acceptable for me and for the people I relate to.

Many of us were brought up to see everything through the frame of responsible, productive, activity. Reframing would give us an opportunity to make other choices.

Failures and Learning Opportunities

Beverley recalls a story about reframing with organizational impact.

I was working with a functional team of about 25 people to help them review their work over the past year, acknowledge what they achieved and refine their operating plan for the following year. The vice president was very enthusiastic about this exercise. She was proud of her team's accomplishments and was anticipating great results. She asked the group to go into their sub groups and prepare a list of their successes and failures and then share their lists with the larger group.

The group looked stunned and horrified. They did not want to follow through with her request. The vice president did not know why she got this reaction and the room stood still. As the facilitator, I suggested we

REFRAME failures to learning opportunities. Immediately there was a collective sigh of relief. The vice president said, "Of course, that is what I meant." The group completed the activity with much enthusiasm and pride, resulting in a great dialogue and discussion that would not have happened without the reframe. This is a great example of how reframing had a triple impact. Level 1, it enabled this VP to be more effective with her *Use-of-Self.* This change resulted in Level 2, the team being more open and productive resulting in Level 3, a strategy that will positively impact the whole organization.

Reflections

Reflection Questions

❏ What are your frames?
❏ What did you do differently as a result of your reframing?
❏ What impact did your reframe have on others?

Resources

Additional Resources

The Journal of Applied Behavioral Science, A Publication of the NTL Institute. Volume 42 Number 3 September 2006. *A Monumental Legacy. The Unique and Unheralded Contributions of John and Joyce Weir to the Human Development Field* by Philip Mix.

This article provides an overview of John and Joyce Wier's legacy in the area of self differentiation. They are the creators of the Percept Framework based on the foundational principles of humanistic psychology and influenced by Abraham Maslow, Carl Rogers, Gestalt Perception Theory and the psychoanalytic concept of transference. Percept Theory challenges the individual to accept maximum responsibility for how they experience themselves in the world. Also included in this article are the references for other readings on this topic.

Concept #3: Power

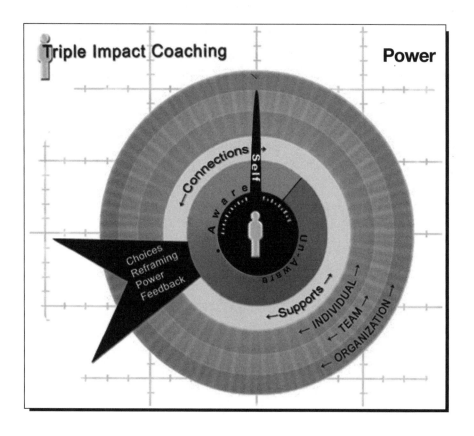

"He who controls others may be powerful, but he who has mastered himself is mightier still"

Lao Tzu
Chinese Taoist Philosopher, founder of Taoism

Being an agent for oneself or being an agent for others by helping them grow and develop is the focus of this concept. We are equating agency to power, owning one's own power or empowering others.

Power plays an important role in coaching and mentoring. It is an interactive concept. We can own it, take it and/or give it away. We can also help others be their own agents or we can take away their agency. All these dynamics can happen through conscious interactions or in ones which we are not aware of what we are doing.

As we mature, we generally move from patiency to agency in striving to achieve our personal and professional goals. Agency is being accountable for our own behavior and helping others become accountable for theirs. Agency is self-determined. The cause and power of choice and action is within one's self, as opposed to being directed and acted on by others.

Agency and its implications form an important *Use-of-Self* concept, at times difficult to grasp. We are often not aware of how subtly someone has taken away our power or agency, or how unwittingly we have given it away. Likewise, we can be unaware of how we take someone else's power or agency away and how clueless they are that we have done so.

One example of giving away our power could be experienced in any meeting where we observe someone interrupting us and finishing our sentences and/or taking our discussions and moving them into another direction.

Another way to lose our agency is when we ourselves give up our power. For example, when we hear in meetings, or elsewhere, that our ideas are being credited to someone else and we do nothing to correct this misattribution, we are giving up our agency. We can just as easily take away someone's agency or power by stepping in and doing for them what they could, and may want or need to do for themselves.

Agency Examples

Scouts & Guides

We can all identify with the boy scout or girl guide who helps a little old lady cross the street. This image has been ingrained in us as a nice, loyal, helpful thing to do. However, it is also based on the assumption that the little old lady needs to be helped across the street. We take away her agency when we try to help when she may be fully capable of crossing on her own and may not want any help. Our scouts can assist her without taking away her agency or her ability to choose by asking if she needs or wants help.

Sometimes people act based on the following beliefs:
By helping others I am saving them or providing them with a much-needed service, something they would be unable to do on their own. It will make them feel good if I let others help me or do favors for me. I can't make any decisions. It's up to them.

Becky and Her Bicycle

Edie recalls a time when she learned about agency through an experience with her daughter.

As a youngster, Becky was not very coordinated and struggled to learn to ride a two-wheeler. As her parents, Charlie and I attempted, with as much care and concern as we could muster, to support her in her struggles. We are both consultants and educators and therefore, certain that our skills and experiences were enough for this task. However, we were getting nowhere. So when a young friend of hers came over for a play day, Charlie and I (thoroughly frustrated and exhausted) went out to lunch to pull ourselves together. When we returned, Becky and her friend Jackie were gleefully riding around and around the garage, each on her own bicycle. Becky's comment to us as she rode by was "Jackie taught me how to ride while you were gone. She could and you couldn't." That was obvious, but what we were curious about was what made the difference? In talking with them, we determined that Jackie role modeled by riding her bike, and she was sure that Becky would catch on and do the same. In contrast, Charles and I stood on the ground and worried that she would never catch on so we tried to ride for her. She did not feel empowered and lost the sense of her own agency. Jackie allowed her to reclaim her agency.

We have found the following exercises very helpful in illustrating this concept.

Exercises

Volunteer Helper Exercise:

Timing	Activity	Responsibilities and Materials
	Warning: This is a brain teaser **Belief system:** The facilitator must be confident that this is important. Participants will not be able to grasp the concept without the exercise. Once they do the exercise it becomes clearer. It can be a very powerful exercise. **Objective:** 1) Learn how you take control of your own choices and actions 2) Learn how you empower or disempower others 3) Learn how you can help others take ownership and act more purposefully.	

Timing	Activity	Responsibilities and Materials
10 min	**Setting the Context:** Give an overview of Agency. Explain that this exercise is an example of someone trying to get someone else to do something. Through this exercise you will learn how you use your own agency to help others to use theirs.	
20 min	**Perform a demonstration.** Ask the group for 2 volunteers *Volunteer #1: Patient* Instruct one volunteer to sit in a chair and pretend to be in pain. Give them these instructions: "You are a patient and it hurts for you to get up out of the chair. You have a broken left arm and just had hip replacement surgery. You are comfortable sitting in the chair. However, it is important for you to get up and move around in order to be healthy and walk again." *Volunteer #2: Helper* The other volunteer's job is to get the patient up out of the chair. Both Volunteers are asked to keep the concepts of agency in mind while performing their assigned tasks. Debrief demonstration	1 chair 2 volunteers: helper, patient
	Facilitator Notes: At this point, the person in the chair usually becomes a long-suffering patient. The helper tries to help by using logic, incentives, support and, in some cases, force. Generally speaking, the harder the helper works to get the patient moving, the more determined the patient becomes not to move, resulting in the helper getting more and more frustrated. We've seen some helpers finally pick up the person to make it happen.	

Timing	Activity	Responsibilities and Materials
	When you see that the pair may be ready to give up, you can suggest the helper let someone else try. This technique often presents different tactics, approaches, or results. When the exercise is completed, you can stop the demonstration and debrief it in the following ways: Sample debrief questions for volunteers. Use the same for group exercise. *Patient:* 1. What were you experiencing during this exercise? 2. Were you empowered? 3. Did you feel like you were in control of your choices, decisions? 4. What were you resisting and why? 5. What did the helper do to get you to move out of your chair? 6. What did they do that hindered your ability to move out of the chair? 7. When do you think you were being empowered? 8. When do you think your agency was being taken away? *Helper:* 1. What were you experiencing during this exercise? 2. What were you attempting to do? 3. What types of resistance did you face? 4. What do you think was going on with your patient? 5. What did you do to help yourself understand what your patient needed? 6. How did you help the patient get out of the chair? 7. What hindered your ability to empower the patient? 8. How much did you influence or control the situation? 9. How much control did you leave with the patient?	

Timing	Activity	Responsibilities and Materials
	Others/observers: 1. What are your observations? 2. How are you experiencing agency? Debrief All: Review any general comments	
15 min	**Group Exercise:** Repeat this exercise with the rest of the group. Divide the group into pairs and facilitate the exercise so that each person has a chance to be the helper and the patient.	
10 min	Afterwards debrief all pairs (patients and helpers). Share results in the large group. *Individual reflections:* Ask everyone to get into pairs and give an example from their own experience of when they either had their agency taken away or took away someone else's agency.	

The debrief of this exercise can be customized to achieve a variety of objectives.

Role and Context:

You may want to review general comments and make links to the participant's application of Agency in their work and role. Beverley used this exercise to look at the role of Human Resources in coaching leaders and managers in organizations. HR was moving from a tactical role to a coaching role where they had to empower and coach their leaders and managers to coach their teams. The exercise helped the HR practitioners to learn about their choices in coaching others and empowering them to act and perform.

In this same exercise we explored the role of resistance to change. The practitioners learned what people needed to adapt to change. As coaches they learned what their people needed to help others to accept and move with change. The HR organization learned the value of

> ❏ listening to understand the other person's issues, concerns and motivations
> ❏ expressing rationale and logic for the change
> ❏ connecting purpose, goals with motivation and meaning
> ❏ understanding their choices during the process and how this helps and hinders others

Reflections

Reflection Questions:

> ❏ How aware are you of your own agency?
> ❏ How aware are you of other people's agency?
> ❏ How do you give and take away agency from others?
> ❏ Do you maintain your own power and accountability or do you let people take it away from you?
> ❏ In what ways do we collude in giving up our agency and/or letting others take it away?

Resources

Additional Resources

Beyond the Wall of Resistance by Rick Maurer (2003)
This book covers unconventional strategies that build support for change.

Managing Resistance to Change or Readiness to Change? by Céline Bareil
Cahiers de recherché du CETO n. 04-02 – January 2004

Six Pillars of Self Esteem by Nathaniel Branden (1993)
Branden talks about personal responsibility and self reliance. His six pillars explore self- efficacy: the power to produce effects or intended results with effectiveness, the belief that you can act, do and succeed in achieving your intentions.

Lyons Markers of Individuation by Denise Lyons. Dissertation, Rutgers University, 2002

Concept #4: Feedback

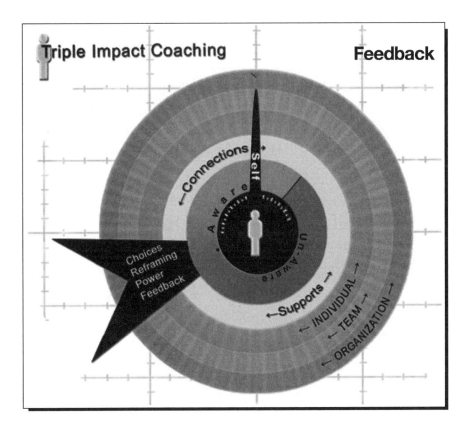

"Like the happy centipede, many people get along fine working with others, without thinking about which foot to put forward. But when there are difficulties, when the usual methods do not work, when we want to learn more - there is no alternative but to examine our own behavior in relation to others."

Joe Luft
Johari Window

Our approach will help you to explore your beliefs about feedback and examine how those beliefs influence your behavior and interactions with others. You will learn to maximize your ability to give and receive feedback; to set up conditions so that you can get the feedback you want; and to explore the dynamics of feedback, applying feedback in team and organizational settings.

We believe that feedback as an educational tool, helps give people control over the choices they make about when and how they choose to change. It puts the power to use the information and change in the hands of the receiver of the message, rather than the giver, as is usually expected.

Some people have a belief system around feedback that sounds like the following: I can't give someone feedback because they will be angry with me. My feedback will hurt someone because they won't want to hear it. Nothing will change. I will put too much stress on the relationship if I give them feedback. Others believe there is no point in asking for feedback because it will make me more vulnerable. I may hear something I don't want to hear. People will see my weaknesses and hold it against me. It will be a career limiting move.

Viewing feedback as an educational tool or learning opportunity takes away the negative connotation that feedback is good or bad and makes the experience more neutral and engaging. If we can look at what we are hearing as pure information and believe that we are in control of how we receive it and understand our interpretation of it, we can decide if it is useful or not. We can go a step further and realize that we are learning about the person giving us feedback. When we are given feedback, we get some idea of how we are being seen by that person. This information may or may not have any relationship to how I see myself, but it gives me another person's perspective.

Choices

The choice of what to do with feedback is always in the control of the receiver. The receiver can distort it, ignore it, save it for the future, swallow it whole or find it useful or not. As the receiver of feedback you have some choices that can set the conditions for success.

Using the e-mail analogy, we will explore these choices:

When you receive feedback that matches your experience you can read it and absorb it. When you receive feedback that does not match your experience you can delete it. Caution: if you get similar feedback from a variety of sources and continually delete it, you may want to look at this message more carefully.

You may get feedback that does not arrive at the right time or place for your consideration, but deserves more follow up, reflection or discussion. In this case you can save it or file it for another time.

Receiving Feedback
You have choices, Feedback is like E-mail. You can...

Feedback always tells something about the giver. When giving feedback, it is important to be aware of what you are telling the receiver about yourself. As the receiver of feedback, you may realize that the feedback message may have very little to do with you, or it may be accurate and relevant about yourself. Feedback always contains information about the person giving the feedback. That's why anonymous feedback has so little relevance. It's out of context, since feedback always reflects how someone is seeing you from their perspective.

Interpretations

As the giver of feedback you don't know how effective you've been in communicating your message, until you check it out. When somebody gives a feedback message, the interpretation of the message is done by the receiver. The receiver has a reaction to the message based on his/her experience and interpretation. The giver may have a reaction to the receiver's reaction. The complexity of this process may explain why the message, after going through all the filters, may not have the effect that the giver intended in the first place. In order for the feedback process to be complete, once again, the giver needs to checkout how the message was received and, if possible, refine the message to make it easier for it to be heard as intended.

It takes a nano-second to go from the message through the interpretation to the reaction and the reaction about the reaction. The giver is left with the final phase, which may or may not have much to do with the intention of the original message.

Relationship of the Giver and Receiver of Feedback

Feedback always tells something about the giver and the receiver. In giving feedback, you choose what to focus on and what is important to you. This results in an expression or interpretation of our own assumptions, values and intentions. Often we don't think of feedback in this full context - including the giver as part of the message. Knowing this helps the receiver sort out how much of the feedback he or she can use and how much just provides information about the giver.

Feedback is a process. The more we disclose about ourselves the more people are able to understand our intentions, and the more others disclose the more we can know about them. The Johari Window is a model developed by Joseph Luft and Harry Ingram and is based on the belief that feedback is essential for effective communication.

The Johari Window
by Joseph Luft and Harry Ingram

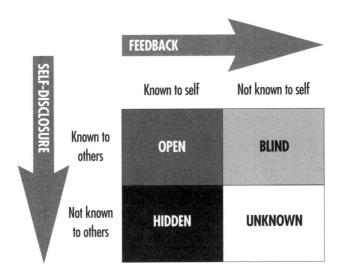

This graphic features four windows or areas that are influenced by our interactions with each other. The upper left window is the Open area which contains information that is known to both myself and to others. For example: You know that our names are Beverley and Edie. The Hidden area (bottom left) is information that is known to us, but not to you. When I disclose to you that Beverley lives in Montreal and Edie lives in Maryland, you now know a little more about us. Our hidden area is a bit smaller and the open area is larger. This information may lead us to have other conversations about your experiences in Montreal or Maryland.

The Blind area (upper right) is information that is not known to us but is known to you. An example that would describe opening the blind area is one that Edie tells about a **Use-of-Self** program that she and Charlie were doing for Senior College participants in Maine. The program was for Sunday evening, all day Monday and Tuesday. On Sunday evening, 20 seniors arrived and settled comfortably in the chairs in the room, most of which were rocking chairs. All evening, as Edie and Charlie lectured and shared their experiences, the participants rocked and smiled enthusiastically, obviously enjoying the evening.

The morning when the participants returned, they came with an important request for Edie and Charlie. They asked if the two of them could talk much louder so that they could be heard. They enjoyed the evening but had not been able to hear most of the information that had been shared. They were too polite to mention it the night before, but after checking with each other, they thought it was important to share this information. This is an example of what was clearly in Edie and Charlie's blind area. They had no idea they weren't being heard by the group. It was only through the feedback that they were able to change their behavior.

Lastly, the Unknown area (bottom right) is information that is unknown to both me and you. This window opens up while we are in interaction with each other. Through our conversations, we may discover similar interests and experiences or insights that come about as a result of our interactions. Beverley called these "AH HA" moments. When this happens we enlarge our open area and reduce the unknown. We once worked with a colleague who had a similar approach to his work in organizational development. At one point in our project, we talked about using a specific exercise to illustrate a point, which led to a discussion that revealed that we had both studied in the same university program. This insight helped us to move faster on our design process because we realized that we had common training and technologies available to us.

As you can see, self-disclosure is a key element in the skill of giving and receiving feedback effectively. We have choices about what we disclose about ourselves and in what contexts and situations we disclose it. As we become more adept at *Use-of-Self*, we become more discriminating about what we choose to disclose, understanding what information will be helpful to the conversation and to the relationship. We also make conscious choices about what not to disclose.

Wrappings

How do you wrap your feedback?
In order to give effective feedback we must be aware of the variety of wrappings. These wrappings may have an impact on how the receiver translates and/or interprets the message. Wrappings come in all sizes: power, motivations and perceptions, from both the receiver and giver of feedback. What is the power relationship between the giver and receiver? What is the emotional state of the giver? What were their intentions and motivations? All of this has an impact on the feedback process.

Contracting for feedback

Feedback is most useful when you are clear about what you want, when you want it and how you want it. This makes the expectations clear for both the giver and the receiver.

Sharing these feedback expectations at the beginning of a group session or team meeting can be very powerful in helping individuals and teams to establish guidelines, principles and norms for creating dialogue, learning or coaching environments.

Now that you understand our principles of giving and receiving feedback, here are a few of our favorite feedback exercises to help you learn about your *Use-of-Self* in giving and receiving feedback. The effectiveness of each of these exercises is dependent on time, purpose and the level of intimacy or respect established in the group.

Exercises

Deliberate Contracting Exercise

Timing 60 min.	Activity	Responsibilities and Materials
5 min	**Instructions** Ask participants in the group to think about their behavior and identify something they would like to get feedback on. **Form trios.**	Paper and pen for observer Trios: giver, receiver, observer
10 min.	Ask participants to select 2 people to work with, one to give feedback, the other to observe. Once participants are settled into their three-person groups, provide the following instructions.	
5 min.	Receiver: Asks the giver to provide them with feedback on their chosen topic in relation to their *Use-of-Self*. Topics might include such issues as how well they communicate, engage others, open their hidden window, etc.	

Timing	Activity	Responsibilities and Materials
	Observers and Givers of Feedback:	
	1. Stick to what you hear from the receivers. Give feedback that is asked for and do not use the exercise as an opportunity to dump on someone.	
	2. Respect the space of the receivers. Stop if they are showing signs of distress. Continue if they are engaged, following, interested and/or curious.	
	3. Be sure the receivers are constantly reminded that they are in control and have choices. They are making a choice about what they want feedback on and how they interpret and act on the feedback.	
	4. Help them reflect and understand what they are learning about the choices they make about their **Use-Of-Self**.	
	Observer: (Optional) The person receiving feedback can assign an observer, someone to take notes for them while feedback is being given to them. This will help them focus on what is being said and enable them to follow up with details after the exercise is completed.	
	While the trios are working, reinforce the following guidelines: The receiver is in control. He or she will tell you what type of feedback they are looking for.	
10 min	Giver gives feedback as per receivers instructions	
10 min	Receiver interprets feedback and discusses with giver. After receiving feedback, the receiver restates the essence of what is being told to them. This helps them check it out and validates that the intention of the message matches what was received. The receivers can then add what they intend to do with the feedback they received.	
10 min	Observers provide information from their observations	

Timing 60 min.	Activity	Responsibilities and Materials
10 min	Begin the debrief by asking the group questions after the first person/round has been completed. You want to find out how the experience went with the first person and each of the roles so you can make adjustments, if needed. You might see people acting a bit resistant because their usual beliefs and experiences, which may include ideas that feedback is not useful, that it's a dumping exercise and people are not authentic when they give feedback. Some believe that people give feedback to fill the need or please the receiver rather than to be helpful to the receiver by pointing out their blind spots.	

Contracting for Coaching Feedback

Feedback is an essential ingredient for the coach and the learner. For both parties to be effective they need to know how to communicate with one another. Exploring the elements of feedback is one way to create this discussion and set the guidelines for their relationship.

In coaching relationships, there is often an implicit contract, especially when the coach is in a formal role of giving feedback to their learner. We find it very helpful in these relationships to set up a formal contract for giving and receiving feedback. Beverley uses the following approach to contract for feedback with her clients.

Whenever I begin a coaching relationship with a new client, I ask them the following questions that help me gain insight into their beliefs and assumptions, and enables them to take control of the feedback process.

❑ What will success look like for you at the end of this coaching program?

❑ How should we give each other feedback as we progress?

❑ Who else do you need feedback from and how and when will you seek it out?

Often we are called to work with clients when communication has broken down, or to help people adjust to their new role or developmental opportunities. Some typical coaching contracts have included coaching people through transition while they adopt their new role, or coaching a leader to work more effectively with their employees. In all these cases, we try to include the client's manager and peers at various points of the coaching process so that we can get feedback related to the clients' current performance and learning objectives. We then coach the client on how to seek out and ask for feedback that is helpful to them. Often coaching is about helping people get the courage to act, frame their words, sort out their feelings, and gain clarity about what exactly they want feedback on, and then help them to develop strategies to get it.

How can you get the feedback that you want?

Beverley tells a story of when she was asked to work with a client to help him develop his communication skills. "After a few weeks he was told that he was not improving. This surprised my client because he believed he was progressing and could list off a number of areas where he was working well with his group. However, he was feeling frustrated because he was lacking specific information about where he was not improving. We worked on helping him to seek out feedback from his boss. After he and his boss had a discussion, he learned some new information. His boss was waiting for a report that my client had delayed producing because he was very busy and didn't think it was a priority. He also did not communicate this assumption to his boss, which resulted in frustration and misunderstanding. This discussion helped my client to be clear on what his boss's expectations were of him. He also learned what was important for his boss to be successful and quickly turned around the report. This conversation created a dialogue between them and cleared the way for open communication and resulted in a win-win. The feedback that my client got from his boss took on a greater meaning than if it came from someone else. In turn, his boss had a greater appreciation of his own lack of communication skills, and then took the initiative to look at his own development opportunities in giving feedback."

These same principles apply to other relationships. We will explore in more detail how to establish and effectively use support systems, our 5th *Use-of-Self* Concept.

Contracting for feedback

We often hear the complaints that I never get feedback. If you want it there are a variety of ways that you can get it if you choose to seek it out. You can create formal and informal feedback opportunities.

Formal contracting is probably the one we are most familiar with. This takes place through performance reviews with your manager, or at project milestones when doing lessons learned, or debrief sessions. It is usually planned, scheduled and influenced by other agendas that are not totally controlled by the receiver.

Informal contracting is, in our opinion, the better way to get feedback. It is available to us all the time. We can have more control of shaping the kind of feedback we need and want. We can obtain feedback at the end of an interaction or meeting by asking how it went and seeking it out.

Support systems are also a great way to help us seek out feedback in a situation that may be more difficult in our work settings. By telling a colleague what you are working on and asking them to observe you in action, and then give you feedback afterward, provides you with a more natural way of obtaining feedback. You can also use your support system to help you plan or role play for practice prior to them observing you in action.

Self observation, rather than wait for others to give you feedback you can also develop the skills and practice to observe yourself by watching the impact your behavior and actions have on others. Keeping a journal is one way to track the themes, patterns and progress of your behavior.

We recommend that rather than wait for a scheduled opportunity, you use every opportunity available to you to get feedback. Remember, feedback tells us a lot about the giver. After you begin making conscious choices and behaving differently, ask yourself if you are seeing differences in your interactions with the person who gave you the initial feedback? Are you still hearing the same complaints from the same people? Are you accomplishing your objectives with the changes that you made in your behavior and actions?

Anonymous feedback has less impact and it also loses its relevance without a context, specific examples and proper timing. Edie and Beverley recall a time when they did a coaching program and got great reviews from the participants. However, one participant rated one section of the program really low and we only found this out after the program. In order for us to understand what this feedback meant, we needed to follow up. We discovered that the individual took the program without knowing that there was a section that related to an area that he was not interested in. Understanding his context and expectations helped us better understand the low score, however, his timing did not help us to adjust the design so that he could more fully participate.

Many times we give and receive anonymous feedback thinking we are communicating well, when in actual fact this may not change anything without relevant follow up and context.

The following exercise is a great way to bring about a deeper awareness of how the receiver is in control of the interpretation of feedback.

Exercises

Control/Interpretations Exercise

Timing 60 min.	Activity	Responsibilities and Materials
	Context Setting: The context setting upfront for this exercise is critical. To set up this exercise, we recommend you speak with your co-trainer or a significant person in the room and not with the group. Tell him or her what you are about to do. Just before implementing the exercise say to the group "This is an exercise only to illustrate a point."	
	Objective To demonstrate that control and interpretation of the feedback lies in the hands of the receiver. **Facilitator:** Turn to your co-trainer or significant person and say: " I wanted you to know that you are doing much better lately"	

Timing	Activity	Responsibilities and Materials
	Stop and then look at the reactions of the group. The group usually reacts in a variety of ways: stunned and shocked that you decided to say this to this person, disbelief or positive because you acknowledged their progress. Turn to the person that you gave the feedback and ask the following questions: 　1. I just gave you a message. What is your interpretation? 　2. How/what did you feel about your interpretation? 　3. How did you feel about your feelings about 　　　your interpretation? You may get a range of interpretations: put down, I felt terrible, feel badly that I feel terrible about either myself or your behavior, that was a nice thing to say, I agree and possibly I feel good about the fact that you said it.	
	Debriefing Rather than debrief what it was that you said, focus on their interpretations. Check out the perceptions of others in the group. Illustrate the learning point that all feedback is subject to interpretation by the receiver and that it is important to check it out. Feedback always reflects the receiver's relationship to the giver.	

All of these exercises can be done in pairs, small groups and large groups. Here is one exercise that you can do in a team or group setting.

Exercises

Team Feedback Exercise:

Timing 60 min.	Activity	Responsibilities and Materials
60 min	This exercise works well at the end of a workshop or session where there is a comfort level of openness and sharing within the group or team. Instruct the group to think about what type of feedback they want, who they would like to get if from and who they would like to give it to. Then ask them to wander around and give and receive feedback. Participants are also instructed to ask permission from the receiver prior to giving feedback. Do this in rounds until it looks like everyone has heard from who they wanted to hear from and vice versa.	

Reflections

Questions for Reflection

❑ Why are you successful in getting feedback?

❑ How can you help others to do the same?

❑ What are your beliefs, assumptions and messages that you carry with you that facilitates your ability to give and receive feedback?

❑ What are your beliefs, assumptions and messages that you carry with you that makes it difficult or hinders your ability to give and receive feedback?

❏ What is blocking you?

❏ Is your belief system different if you give it to a person in authority, peer, subordinate or family member?

Resources

Resources

What Did You Say? The Art of Giving and Receiving Feedback by Charles Seashore, Edith Whitfield Seashore and Gerald Weinberg. (1996)
Understanding the psychology of giving and receiving feedback.

The Johari Window:A Graphic Model of Awareness in Interpersonal Relations by Joseph Luft (1982)
NTL Reading Book for Human Relations Training

Concept #5: Support Systems

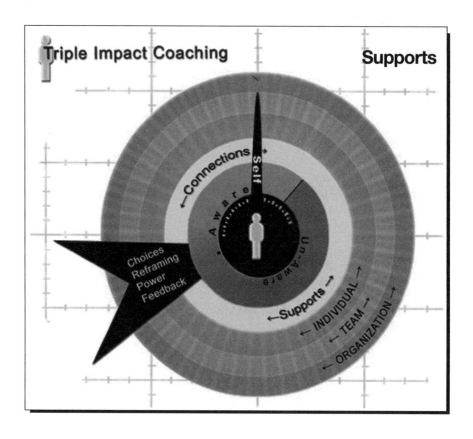

"Tis not enough to help the feeble up, but to support him after"

William Shakespeare
Poet and Playwright
1564-1616

Building support systems for ourselves, which will enable us to be more effective at whatever we want to accomplish, does not usually occur to us. Moreover, helping our clients build support systems for themselves also does not occur to us or to them. In fact, it is difficult for most of us to ask for and seek support. This is often perceived or believed to be a sign of weakness. Actually if you think about it, very little is accomplished alone. Support is often needed and actually required to make things happen and sustain our learning and growth.

Early in life, we were taught to believe that we should be able to do things ourselves, or if we were to ask for support, we wouldn't get the support we wanted or needed, or that our request would be dismissed or rejected. On the otherhand, another belief system many of us maintain is that if we were asked to support someone, we would be more than happy to do it. In fact, we might find joy in using our expertise, knowledge and abilities and would definitely make ourselves available to help out. We seem to hold two conflicting beliefs about support systems.

To recognize our reluctance to seek support is a beginning. To actually get the kind of support we need requires more thoughtful action. When our clients are in need of support, they are often stuck, feeling overwhelmed, procrastinate and are sometimes resentful. Much of our coaching in this area is focused on helping others to help themselves.

Here is an exercise to help you and your clients understand support systems. The exercise is comprised of two parts:

Part 1: Understanding our beliefs about support systems, and

Part 2: Building and sustaining support systems.

Exercises

Support Systems Exercise

Timing	Activity	Responsibilities and Materials
Reflections	**Part 1: Understanding our beliefs about support systems** **Objective:** Explore and understand my beliefs about seeking and using supports. **Reflections:** Individually write down your answers to the following questions: 1. What were your early messages about seeking support? 2. Who gave you these messages? 3. What are your beliefs about support systems that resulted from these early messages? 4. What beliefs do you hold today? 5. How do these beliefs help or hinder your effectiveness? **Discussion:** In small groups In pairs or trios, share your reflections on the questions. Talk about your common beliefs, themes or patterns about support systems that you would like to share with your group. **Debrief:** Large Group We then share our thoughts about support systems and their significance in helping us accomplish our goals to bring about change, sustain our learning and growth and also how we Use our Self to empower others to do the same.	

Timing	Activity	Responsibilities and Materials
	Part 2: Building support systems and sustaining learning and growth **Objective:** Create an understanding of our current support systems and develop one that will sustain us in achieving our objectives. Present the following Support Systems Model to help participants broaden their understanding of their current support systems and help them build the one that they need.	

Support Systems Model
by Charles Seashore

According to Charles Seashore, a support system is a resource pool drawn on selectively to support me in moving in a direction of my choice, which leaves me stronger. The following is his model that has been very effective building a variety of support systems.

EXPERIENCE	SUPPORT TYPE	OUTCOME
Confusion	Role Models	Clarity
Isolation	Common Interests	Social Contacts
Aloneness	Friend	Intimacy-Caring
In Crisis	Action-Oriented	Supported
Self Esteem	Affirm Strength	Confidence
Disconnection	Referral Agents	Connections
Plateau	Challengers	Cutting Edge

As we explain the dimensions of the matrix, we ask each participant to reflect upon and write down who or what comes to them as someone or something that would fit into that category of support for them.

❏ Explain the components of the model in detail.
❏ Provide examples of each.
❏ Working in the same small groups as Step 1, ask them to share their views of their current support system. Identify who is missing? Who is overused as a support? Who needs to be included to help them achieve their objectives?

Role Model: In one sense we all may be role models, even though we may be unaware of who has chosen us to be that part of their support system. For all of us, at sometime, someone was a role model whose support we could continue to call on even if that person was no longer on earth. Beverley and Edie still recall words of wisdom from mentors who continue to sustain and influence them. Growing up, Beverley was mentored by her parish priest who later became Bishop of Montreal. His name was Father Willard. When facing an ethical dilemma she will often say to herself, what would Father Willard say? It helps her to process the situation and explore other possibilities that she may not have thought about in the moment.

Common Interests: Major support structures are the gatherings of people with common interests. It is astounding that, in our society, there seems to be a group for anyone needing support for almost anything. For example, Alcoholics Anonymous, Breast Cancer Survivors, Single Parents, etc. A few years ago when Edie's daughter went to Israel on a two month anthropological trip, she chose to stay for a year to attend a Yesiva. Edie's concern was that she would choose to stay in Israel for the rest of her life as lots of young people were doing at that time. Edie shared her concern with a group she was consulting and they informed her that there was, near her home, a group of parents who met regularly to talk about their children who went to Israel and stayed. At various times, in everyone's life, it's enlightening to meet with others who are experiencing common interests or concerns.

Friend: How do you define "friend?" The closest we have come to a definition is someone who will be there for you no matter how much trouble you get into. Everyone needs at least one of these supports in their life.

Action-Oriented: Often we don't know before a crisis who we might call on at that time. Edie recalls a time she was called when someone was in a crisis. She got the call because the person experienced her as someone who would take action fast and make things happen to handle the crisis in an appropriate way. It's useful to have action-oriented people in your support system.

Affirm Strength: There are times when we have lost, if only momentarily, our self-esteem, and need in our support system someone who can help affirm our strengths. Edie recalls saying only two crucial sentences to someone who called her in the midst of a struggle with low self-esteem. Edie's reply was, "Sally, remember who you are. I do and you must." It is important to have someone support you at that time to recall your competencies and strengths and help you get back on your feet.

Referral Agents: Among the most important support in any system is an informal referral agent, a resource to help you access goods, services, knowledge and supports. This type of support is often needed when people are in new situations, such as a move to a new neighborhood, joining a new organization, changing careers or making life changes. These resources open doors, put in a good word, recommend the right people to help you fulfill your needs. Often the best support you can provide is to help others find the best resource for their specific needs.

Challenger: Perhaps the most lacking element in someone's support system is the Challenger. As we continue to change and grow, a lot of our current support systems begin to act differently. They would like us to stay the same. In this way we are familiar to them but we may plateau in our development. When we develop, it is necessary for us to build new supports to help us sustain our growth. We don't need to abandon our old support system, if we had one, rather we can benefit from broadening and expanding our support system to include new and challenging supports who will stretch us, help us think out of our boxes, and introduce us to new ways of being. Often, we outgrow parts of our previous support system because they are not up to date or current with our context, goals and objectives. It is important to have people in our support system who continue to challenge us to keep growing.

Non-Human Supports: We talk mostly about people as supports, but other very important supports are non-human, such as animals, music, exercise, technology, books, nature and hobbies. Often we need the support of a companion or a resource to access one of these non-human support systems.

Following this exercise, many participants become aware and concerned about how few supports they have, or, in some cases, how grateful they are for the support they now realize that they do have. Others also realize that they over use or under use some of their supports.

Before we end the session, we often ask if anyone would like help in beginning to build some parts of their support system. We ask them if they would like to choose anyone in the group to help them begin this process. Many people take advantage of this opportunity. To help them get started we ask them to tell us the support they would like and from whom they would like it and then the exchange begins.

As with all of our activities, the Triple Impact concept is very important in building support systems. We first need to understand our own belief system and how we get support for ourselves so that we can bring our own system up-to-date. This helps us to be more effective in helping others realize how important support systems are for them, and then we can more effectively help those we work with do the same for others. Support systems are essential in helping us sustain the new learning we are acquiring, the changes we are making and the work we are doing.

Reflections

Reflections:

❑ Who is in your support system?
❑ Do you have all the supports you need?
❑ If not, who and what do you need?
❑ How will you seek out the support you need to be at your best?

Resources

Additional Resources:

Developing and Using a Personal Support System by Charles Seashore. NTL Reading Book for Human Relations Training 1982 NTL Institute.

Concept #6: Connections

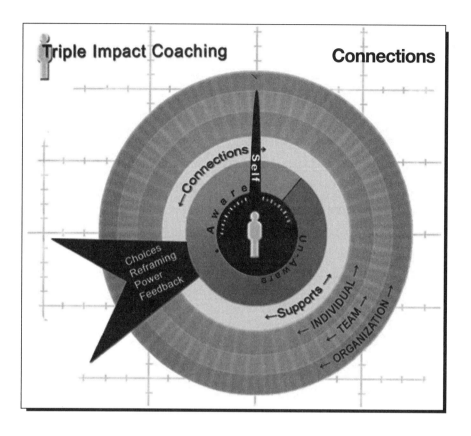

"This kind of education is not about taking steps up to the top of some mountain, where everything can finally be seen, so much as about working together to create a fine cloth. Integration has to take place as we combine individual and collective efforts, interconnecting the fibers of different ideas. The resulting cloth is certainly woven, but by no particular thread so much as by every single one, by every single idea and experience discussed in that classroom."

Henry Mintzberg
Managers not MBA's

Beverley and Edie have worked all of their careers using systems approaches like family systems theory and whole scale change. All of these theories reinforce the principle that you can't change one part of the system without changing the whole. You can't change one part of the system without understanding the connections, influences and dependencies of the whole. Understanding the connections of the individual or team in their organizational context is essential in providing the best possible coaching experience and is the only way to ensure a Triple Impact.

Recently Beverley was introduced to the Knots Theory quite by accident. She was developing her logo for her business and someone suggested a knot as a visual image. At first, she thought of negative images: tangles, wound up, stuck and frustrated, which are often the feelings that people in new coaching relationships experience. Then she thought of some positive images: loosening, secure, dependable, untangling, reshaping, redesigning, beautiful keltic designs and patterns. Knots also provide safety and security for sailors whose lives depend on them. Are these not consistent with the objectives and hopefully end results of coaching?

This intrigued her and after some research she discovered that people have been researching knots for over 100 years. Scientists such as Gauss, Listing, Kirkman, Tait, and Little have been studying the mathematical formula and the implications of Knots Theory on physics and biology.

For at least the last decade we have been struggling with working in matrices. The key challenges in this type of work setting is understanding how to influence each other without proper authority. Infighting, conflict and silos get reinforced and cross functional teamwork becomes more and more difficult. Imagine if we were to look instead at working together in empowering, responsible and accountable knot formations. We are interdependent. Our survival counts on us providing a key role, support and function in order to be our best, perform and possibly even have fun.

Much of our coaching work is helping people who are in knots to become untangled but, in order to do this, we must first understand the knot. In organizations, these knots have patterns and connections to the bigger whole. We must understand how they are tied together and for what purpose. Are they held together for dear life or are they loose and need to be readjusted or reconfigured to strengthen another adjoining knot?

INDIVIDUAL   TEAM   ORGANIZATION

To get us started, here are a few key questions to help you understand the connections that are relevant for the coaching experience. We ask these questions to give us a sense of where we are starting, what exists and/or needs to be developed.

- ❑ Why are we doing this program? What are the opportunities, challenges and risks?
- ❑ What is the benefit for the individual, team and organization?
- ❑ Who are we developing?
- ❑ How does coaching support the:
    - Business Objectives
    - Vision
    - Values
    - Principles
- ❑ What connections, if any, need to be made and how?
- ❑ What are the measures of success?
- ❑ Are there key strategic initiatives that need to be considered?

❏ Are there any key milestones, factors or influences that can positively or negatively impact the coaching experience?

❏ What is my role as coach in working with the internal partners: participant's direct manager, their team, HR, etc.?

❏ What type of information will be shared outside of the coaching sessions? When? How?

❏ What type of supports are in place to sustain the learning and development for this individual and/or team?

❏ How will feedback be given to the participant, coach and other key stakeholders?

Exercises

Broken Squares Exercise

The following is an exercise that we use to help people understand the interpersonal connections and interdependencies within a team. This exercise has been around for a long time. Beverley and Edie are not sure who was the founder or designer. However, they both remember Henry Malcolm being the first person to share the game with them. The puzzle is as follows:

Each Square is 6 x 6 inches

Place puzzle pieces into 5 envelopes containing the following pieces:
AAAC, GBFC, IHE, DF, AJ
Each participant should be given one envelope to begin the game.

Objectives:

This exercise illustrates the essentials of teamwork. In order to be successful in this game you need to be connected to your team members, communicate, share information and work interdependently.

Instructions:

Introduce the exercise to the team.

Explain the objectives and rationale.

Tell them that this is an exercise in teamwork with two important objectives.

At the end of the game each player on the team must have a six inch square (6-in by 6-in) assembled in front of them.

The game is finished when everyone has their square.

Setting:

This game can be played on the floor or at a small table. Make sure that each team of five has a space where they can sit around to play the game. If you are going to play this game with more than one team at the same time, make sure that there is room to move around, and space so that the teams don't get in each other's way.

Optional: Sometimes we have people observe the teams while playing the game to help them debrief the exercise.

Distribute Puzzle Pieces:

Place the envelopes containing the broken squares on the table and instruct the teams not to look into the envelopes until the game begins.

Explain and post the Broken Squares rules.

BROKEN SQUARES RULES

I. TO WIN

Five (5) complete squares.
Equal size.
One in front of each player.

GAME COMPLETE: When all teams are finished

II. THE CHALLENGE

1. One envelope for each player;
2. Pieces may not make square;
3. Some transfer needed.

III. RULES FOR TRANSFERRING PIECES

DON'TS
1. NO TALKING – SIGNALING;
2. NO GRABBING – DUMPING.

DO'S
1. OFFER – HOLD OUT TO ANOTHER;
2. ACCEPT – OR DECLINE PIECE OFFERED.

Instruct the teams that the five team players cannot talk or communicate with one another in any way, shape or fashion, and that you, the facilitator, will watch them very carefully to see that they abide by this rule. (Be playful with them on this!)

Players cannot simply reach out and take pieces that they think they might need. They must sit quietly and receive pieces from other players. But they cannot take pieces. Teams are also told not to pool all their pieces in the middle of the table so as to construct their five squares. Every player is responsible for his or her own square.

A team consists of five players who play the game only with their own team of five. They do not play with other teams, except perhaps to compete between teams to see which team completes the exercise first.

Coaching

Coaching Tips

It helps sometimes if the teams are made up of people who, when they cannot talk, actually work together as team members in the work place. You can play the game with one team of 5 people or multiple teams of 5. The elements of competition and speed surface when you include more than one team.

As a facilitator, you can adjust your objectives to reflect your current team realities or future expectations by stating that there is a time factor, or an incentive for the first group to finish, or you can also state that there is no deadline or timeline and that the game will finish when everyone is finished. You can watch for and debrief what the groups do when they are finished. Do they observe the others? What impact does this have on the group being observed? What happens when your group finishes first? Do you put pressure on others? Do they put pressure on themselves? What impact does this have on them individually? On the team's performance? You can have a lot of fun with this exercise but we caution you to be clear about what your objectives are for the debrief in order to ensure it achieves the overall objectives of the learning experience.

Comments that you might hear from players:

- ❏ Once my square is finished I am no longer needed in the team.
- ❏ My part of the task is completed.
- ❏ If I accomplish my part everyone will succeed.
- ❏ I am no good at puzzles so I will be a liability to the team in this exercise.
- ❏ I am good at puzzles and can take over and do it for the team.
- ❏ I can do whatever it takes. Break the rules to win if necessary.
- ❏ There is no way we can break the rules. We have to play by the rules.
- ❏ There is a trick, a secret formula to this. The facilitators are setting us up. They are not to be trusted.
- ❏ Are we 5 individuals or a team?
- ❏ What is my contribution?

Warning:

This exercise can be stressful on the facilitator so, for your own comfort, we recommend that you count the pieces beforehand to avoid room for error and then be prepared. Stick with it as this exercise has many opportunities for learning.

Other suggestions for setting up this exercise.

We use this exercise to teach people how to coach others and also to learn about how they lead groups. If this is your objective, you can ask for observers who would watch specific players and then give them feedback on their behavior and the group's process in achieving the objectives. If you are going to use observers, you can position them as the referees who are there to also ensure they play by the rules.

You can also ask the observers, later in the debrief, about how they felt in the observer role. How was this experience similar or different for them in terms of their role at work? Managers or directors often have the strategy in mind but are not hands on for execution. They need to motivate and coach others for performance. How did this exercise help them or hinder their ability to do this? What did they learn about themselves in this role? How did they manage their expectations?

Debrief Guide

The following questions are intended to be a guide for your debrief. Feel free to add your observations and feedback that you think may help the team learn about their performance.

Individual focus on *Use-of-Self*:

❑ What choices did you make?
❑ How did you get in the way of the team's progress?
❑ What did you do to facilitate the team's progress?

Team focus:

❏ What helped or hindered your ability to be successful?

❏ What did others do that enabled or prevented you from achieving your objective?

❏ What helped or hindered your team's ability to be successful?

❏ Any other observations or comments?

❏ Was your behavior in this exercise typical of your behavior in your team?

Coaches/Observers:

❏ What did you observe that can help the team better understand their performance?

❏ Do you have any specific feedback for them as individuals?

❏ How did you feel when you saw what was happening and could not communicate or influence their performance?

❏ What was it like refereeing this team?

❏ What similarities or differences did this exercise have with your real work experience?

❏ Any other observations, comments or suggestions?

Application to work teams:

❏ What happened to your team when others were finished?

❏ Did their behavior help or hinder your team's performance?

❏ What did your team do once they were finished?

❏ How does your experience in this exercise reflect your desire to work as one team?

❏ What are some of your takeaways from this exercise that you would like to apply in your work team?

Later in Chapter 6 we will show you how to develop a Triple Impact Coaching Program and explain in further detail how to make the right connections. In Chapter 7 we will demonstrate the results.

Reflections

Reflection Questions:

> o How connected are you in your day-to-day?
> o Who do you interact with most of the time?
> o Who do you need to be connected to?
> o What choices do you have to be connected or not?

Resources

Additional Resources:

Built To Last. Successful Habits of Visionary Companies by James Collins and Jerry Porras (1994)
Great book about leading with vision. The book explores the theory of core ideology and is filled with examples and case studies.

Managers Not MBA's. by Henry Mintzberg (2004)
A hard look at the soft practice of managing and management development.

The Dance of Change. The Challenges to Sustaining Momentum in Learning Organizations. by Peter Senge, Art Kleiner, Charlotte Roberts, Richard Ross, George Roth and Bryan Smith. (1999)
A great resource for articles, exercises, references, etc. related to change.

The Fifth Discipline Fieldbook. Strategies and Tools For Building A Learning Organization by Peter Senge, Richard Ross, Bryan Smith, Charlotte Roberts, Art Kleiner (1994)
Wonderful resource of exercises, theory and applications.

Chapter 5: Putting it all Together

Sample Triple Impact Coaching: *Use-of-Self* Workshop

The following workshop is a sample of how the exercises might look in a two-day program.

DAY 1

Timing	Activity
DAY 1	
9:00 to 9:10	**Opening Comments** **Greetings**
9:10 to 9:40	**Check In** Introduce yourself by telling us your name and why you chose to come to this program. You might also want to tell us something interesting that you would like us to know about yourself.
9:40 to 9:50	**Agenda** Overview of 2 Days Design Elements: Your will experience a combination of experiential exercises, reflections, theory and practice to help you with your learning. Today's objectives Overview of binder Housekeeping: times for lunch and breaks, washrooms, etc.
9:50 to 10:05	***Use-of-Self*** **: Triple Impact Coaching** Model Concepts Coaching Process
10:05 to 10:20	**Break**
10:20 to 11:40	**Appreciative Interviews (Any coaching experience)** Catch the spirit and essence of what people say. It's not important to catch details Practice listening skills and what it is like to walk in someone else's shoes.

Timing	Activity
DAY 1 (cont.)	
11:40 to 12:00	**The Difference Between Coaching and Mentoring**
12:00 to 1:00	**Lunch**
1:00 to 3:00	**MBTI (Exercises not included)** Intro and Overview Exercises for each dimension Debrief *Use-of-Self* and choices
3:00 to 3:15	**Break**
3:15 to 4:00	**Power: Agency & Self Efficacy** Helper Exercise
4:00 to 4:45	**Introduction to Types of Support Systems** Support for Self Reflection Questions in Learning Partners Think about your own coaching project/or what you learned about yourself today that may influence your ability to coach or mentor others. How do you want to work on this during the course? What do you want to share with others about how you would like others to help you in your learning?
4:45	**Recap**
4:45 to 5:00	**Check Out**

DAY 2

Timing	Activity
DAY 2	
9:00 to 9:25	**Check In**
9:25 to 9:30	**Agenda**
9:30 to 11:00	**Reframing**
11:00 to 12:00	**Let Your Fingers Do The Talking** Debrief: *Use-of-Self* (choices)
12:00 to 1:00	**Lunch**
1:00 to 3:00	**Appreciating Differences** Diversity
3:00 to 3:15	**Break**
3:15 to 3:45	**Feedback**
3:45 to 4:00	**Connections**
4:00 to 4:45	**Individual Coaching Scenario Work & Learning partners** Supports for coaching others to build supports How can you help others/the person you are working with build their own support systems?
4:45	**Recap**
4:45 to 5:00	**Check Out**

PART 3
COACHING IN ACTION

Included in this section are our development process and team coaching program, 3 case studies, advice from our clients and the lessons learned to help you align and position your Triple Impact Coaching Program for success.

Our case studies demonstrate how Triple Impact Coaching helps to build leadership and coaching capacity on an individual, team and organizational level in three Canadian organizations and explores how to create the conditions for success that produce results that will last over time.

The President of Proceco, a Montreal, Quebec based international manufacturing company, used Triple Impact Coaching to support his Management Team to develop their people strategy required to grow a small company into a mid-sized organization.

VIA Rail used Triple Impact Coaching to help a newly formed cross functional leadership team examine an organizational issue: customer focus. The Power of the Team helped create commitment and synergy across the organization that resulted in sustained changes in culture and mindset.

Transcontinental Media used Triple Impact Coaching to transform their Human Resources Department from a technical expert to a business partner by developing their *Use-of-Self* in their coaching, consulting and change agent roles.

Each of these examples will illustrate the benefits of the focus on *Use-of-Self* in Triple Impact Coaching.

Lessons learned will also be provided to help you apply this approach in your own organizations.

Chapter 6: Coaching Program Development Process
    ❑ Triple Impact Coaching Process
    ❑ Sample Team Coaching Program

Chapter 7: Case Studies: Reflections & Lessons Learned
    ❑ Proceco Coaching for Change
    ❑ VIA Rail - The Power of the Team
    ❑ Transcontinental Media - HR Transformation

Chapter 6: Coaching Program Development Process

Triple Impact Coaching requires a disciplined developmental approach. Your approach needs to be customized to adapt to your organizational culture. It will be dependent upon the complexity of your organization, the urgency of your objectives and timeline, the number of people involved and the level of commitment and readiness within the organization. However, it is our experience that regardless of these factors, all steps are required to effectively develop and implement successful coaching programs that lead to sustainable behavioral changes. The following diagram: Triple Impact Coaching Process highlights the main activities that are essential in the coaching program development process. It is followed by a sample Team Coaching Program diagram.

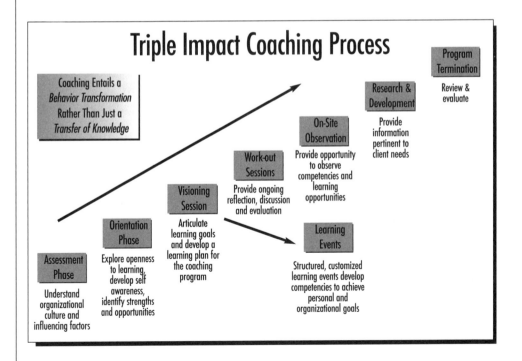

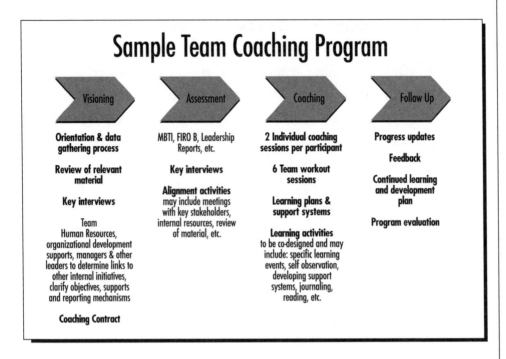

Sample Team Coaching Program

Visioning	Assessment	Coaching	Follow Up
Orientation & data gathering process	**MBTI, FIRO B, Leadership Reports, etc.**	**2 Individual coaching sessions per participant**	**Progress updates**
			Feedback
Review of relevant material	**Key interviews**	**6 Team workout sessions**	**Continued learning and development plan**
Key interviews	**Alignment activities** may include meetings with key stakeholders, internal resources, review of material, etc.	**Learning plans & support systems**	**Program evaluation**
Team Human Resources, organizational development supports, managers & other leaders to determine links to other internal initiatives, clarify objectives, supports and reporting mechanisms		**Learning activities** to be co-designed and may include: specific learning events, self observation, developing support systems, journaling, reading, etc.	
Coaching Contract			

Alignment

This development process and team coaching program ensures your coaching activities are aligned with your organization's vision, strategic priorities and objectives. Alignment gives the program credibility and creates buy-in from the key stakeholders which is required to ensure the program's long-term success. Wherever possible, coaching programs should build on existing work or initiatives. For example, your business case should make explicit the links to your organization's context, leadership development and succession planning initiatives.

Including key stakeholders in designing and developing coaching programs ensures faster integration with the organizational culture and helps facilitate change because everyone will be going through the process together. They will learn how to help and coach each other through the changes. For these reasons, it is very important to understand the needs of your stakeholders. Who are the people that need to be involved? Who will be impacted? How will they be impacted? What level of the organization needs to be included in the process? What support will they need to participate? What are their hopes, wishes, worries and concerns? The very process that you take to identify these stakeholders will go a long way in helping you and your team to clarify the goals of your coaching program.

Here are our six tips on how to ensure alignment based on examples from our case studies.

❏ **Build collaborative processes** in program design by making sure the key stakeholders are consulted and involved throughout the process.

At Transcontinental, the vice president of human resources ensured that the human resources management team was involved in the design, needs assessment, action planning and implementation of the program. She also aligned her plan with the corporate human resources strategy by consulting with the senior vice president of human resources throughout the process.

❏ **Ensure the structure, resources and decision-making processes** are in place to sustain the program.

At Proceco, the President was very active in promoting and communicating his vision and rationale for the coaching program that was designed to help them develop their people strategy to support their changes. He made sure the company had access to the coach when needed and he himself reinforced the principles, philosophy and new behaviors that he was trying to instill in the company.

❏ **Link the program to other organizational strategies** in order to ensure consistency and integration.

The VIA ALP team and the coach worked with the vice president strategy, vice president human resources and director organizational development to transfer theory into practice. By researching the importance of customer focus within VIA, they discovered a key link with cross-functional teams through the service teams. This insight helped them to target the right audience to position their work and obtain buy-in that would lead to critical changes throughout the organization. In addition, many concepts, tools, approaches and resources were used in other internal leadership development programs.

❏ **Create opportunities for learning and development** at all levels of the organization to ensure faster, deeper and lasting change.

By developing their coaching and consulting competencies, the HR Team at Transcontinental was able to put to action right away their learning from their *Use-of-Self* workshop. HR is a valued player in management meetings and is actively engaged in helping the business adapt and adjust to change. They developed an Operations Board Game that management and functional teams are using to examine people and HR related issues. They are successful in building partnerships with their internal customers by coaching and supporting them in the transformation journey. The organization is learning at every level within this organization. They are valued business partners.

❏ **Create internal and external networks and partnerships** for learning and growth. VIA used the McGill Advanced Leadership Program (ALP), friendly consultants, the coach and internal resources to help them to be objective while they were looking in the mirror. This combination of resources and the variety of experiences, tools and techniques helped them validate what was working well within their organization and made explicit the strengths and areas of pride that they wanted to capture and leverage as they moved forward with their customer focus issue.

❏ **Embed the program in overall change management and communication strategies** to help motivate and sustain the momentum of your initiatives.

All case studies spent a significant amount of time and energy making sure their coaching programs supported the key strategic changes and complexities of their organizations. Key messages and validation of the new behaviors and ways of working were communicated regularly to various stakeholders to reinforce the progression towards their goals and desired changes. They also highlighted the success stories which made the journey more meaningful and engaging for everyone.

Including key stakeholders in designing and developing coaching programs will ensure faster integration into the organizational culture and will help facilitate change. Follow Table 2: Coaching Program Alignment Checklist before you embark on a Triple Impact Coaching journey to ensure your program is aligned with your organizational objectives.

Table 2: Coaching Program Alignment Checklist

Essential Support Mechanisms	Yes	No
1. Business Case & Objectives ❏ Do you understand the business case/objectives for your program? ❏ Are they clearly understood by everyone?		
2. The Team ❏ Do you have a champion and a sponsor for your program? ❏ Does everyone know their role in supporting the objectives?		
3. Key Stakeholders ❏ Have you included the key people in your development and design process? ❏ Have you got all the following information? ❒ Who will be critical to the success of your program? ❒ Who will be needed to get your program off the ground? ❒ Who will be required to keep it going? ❒ What are their hopes, wishes, worries and concerns?		
4. Decision Making ❏ Are the structures, resources and decision-making processes in place to sustain the program?		
5. Connections ❏ Is the program connected to other organizational strategies to ensure consistency and integration?		
6. Supports ❏ Have you created internal and external networks and partnerships to support learning on the individual, team and organizational levels?		
7. Communication ❏ Do you have key messages and ways to capture success and learning opportunities?		
8. Evaluation ❏ Do you have a process to capture measures of success? ❏ Do you have a method to capture learning and development at all levels of the organization?		

These three case studies reveal the journey of the *Use-of-Self* in the Triple Impact Coaching process.

Learn how Proceco's President used Triple Impact Coaching to lead his team through growth and change. Learn about how VIA used Triple Impact Coaching with a cross functional leadership team to explore a company wide issue and customer focus, and explore how the vice president of human resources at Transcontinental Media led her team to evolve towards a human resources business partner.

All three companies achieved change that crossed functional boundaries and addressed complex organizational dynamics that resulted in sustainable change. The benefits to their team and organization will be explored along with their unique challenges, insights and advice for anyone wanting to embark on this journey.

We will also explore the coach's reflections that will highlight the importance of building partnerships to successfully implement coaching programs.

Chapter 7: Case Studies: Reflections & Lessons Learned

Case Study # 1: Proceco - Coaching for Change

Proceco engineers and manufactures integrated cleaning systems for manufacturing industries. The company was founded and headquartered in Montreal, Quebec, Canada in 1975. It has approximately 125 employees and over $20,000,000 in sales. Proceco has sales offices in Canada and the US and export about 75% of its products worldwide.

Robert Burns has been President since 2002 and an employee of the company for over 25 years. In 2001, just prior to Burns' promotion to the presidency, Proceco deployed a strategic plan to differentiate itself from its traditional business which was quickly approaching maturity. Just as things started to turn around for the company, two unforeseen events seriously impacted the company's sales: 1) the aftermath of 911 pushed the already distressed aerospace industry, a key market for Proceco, into decline, and 2) a rapidly rising Canadian dollar reduced the company's competitiveness. Proceco's work orders dropped significantly to the point that the company's employees were working at half capacity. The sales team became de-motivated. Sales strategies that worked in the past were ineffective. Employees were misaligned, internal power struggles were building and silos were becoming entrenched. Without losing sight of its strategic direction, severe measures with an emphasis on increasing sales, reducing costs and getting orders out as fast as possible were put into action. Robert's leadership at that time was characterized as task oriented, authoritative and autocratic.

In 2005 Proceco could see the benefits of the strategic turn around. Sales increased and by January 2006 the company had a record backlog of orders. Robert decided in September of 2005 that he needed to do things differently to lead Proceco through the next stage of growth. Previously, he was successful as an operational leader, but now he needed to work out of his comfort zone and be more strategic and coach and empower others to act. The results of an employee survey also revealed that the employees felt overworked and unmotivated. They thought communication was lacking and they were frustrated with the ineffective planning, which was creating a culture of firefighting and a loss of work life balance. Robert knew he would have to influence his senior management colleagues to buy into a new vision and obtain their active support in making change happen at Proceco. To meet these challenges, he signed up for a coaching course with Beverley and Edie at McGill's International Executive Institute. Through the course he learned about the Triple Impact Coaching Model and wanted to use it in his company. He participated in a six-month coaching program as a support to help him lead and coach others through the changes required to bring the company through the next phase of its transition.

The following Challenges, Approach and Results chart explains how fast and deep Robert went with his interventions. Following the chart is an interview with Robert about his coaching experience and his thoughts about using the Triple Impact Coaching Model at Proceco.

Proceco

Challenge:
- ❑ International manufacturing company
- ❑ Small company moving to midsize,
- ❑ Next phase of growth: standardized processes, project management office (PMO), change leadership, human resource strategy, customer focus Priority
- ❑ Complex engineering products requires skilled technical talent
- ❑ High staff commitment
- ❑ Want to be positioned for success

Approach:
- ❑ President took Triple Impact Coaching Program McGill
- ❑ Committed to leadership development, his own and his Management Team
- ❑ Conducted Myers Briggs type inventory workshop
- ❑ Provided weekly onsite coaching to president and management team
- ❑ Developed mechanisms for feedback

Results:

Understanding and commitment to the vision and strategic direction
- ❑ Conducted strategic alignment workshop with all managers
- ❑ Implementing strategy to create a customer focus mindset
- ❑ Objectives are aligned and understood by all
- ❑ Confidence in leadership and their role in supporting the direction

New Structure
- ❑ Implementing new PMO structure strategic hiring & succession planning

People Strategy
- ❑ Developed and implementing a leadership profile: values, competencies
- ❑ Conducted performance reviews & interview process using new approach
- ❑ Conducting leadership development program
- ❑ Completed MBTI for all management team and project managers
- ❑ Motivated and empowered workforce

Robert Burns participated in a dialogue with participants in a *Use-of-Self* Workshop hosted by the Ottawa Organizational Development Network in Ottawa Ontario where he shared his answers to the following questions about his coaching experience.

❑ **What are your accomplishments, challenges and *Use-of-Self* defining moments?**

Initially, I thought of coaching as a technique to teach me how to better understand the coachee and what makes them tick. This is important, no doubt, but coaching taught me something even more important—to better understand myself and how I can affect behavioral changes through my own actions. Coaching helped me to better understand the impact of my behavior on others and the ripple effect that this has on my organization. I now have a more profound understanding of the impact of my behavior and how to more effectively manage my Self for the benefit of the whole.

My greatest accomplishment is my ability to create alignment, buy-in and active support of the management team around the vision and strategic direction.

My challenges are leading and managing the required adjustments in staffing and the ripple effect that is involved with these types of changes. I value commitment and teamwork. I find it very difficult when people leave the company as a result of the changes.

So far, my *Use-of-Self* defining moments occurred when I put myself out there and talked about the vision and strategic direction. We developed a collaborative process to design an all-employee meeting which helped me get my finger on the pulse as well as educate the managers one-on-one, and as a management team, throughout the process. This approach was new for me and my team. However, it enabled me to understand areas of concern, resistance and support. We built in a process to obtain feedback after each step of the process, from every level of the company. This very positive approach continues today and is helping me to be more supportive, empowering and responsive to the needs of the employees.

Another defining moment occurred during an alignment workshop. We brought together all levels of management to roll out the vision and obtain clarity of roles and responsibilities. I was open to the concept but needed coaching to let others speak and not control the meeting. When I let go of control, I was surprised to see that 80% of the management team was aligned without my influence. They were also able to confront the reluctant 20% and develop action plans to address some key issues and concerns. This was a huge learning experience for me. I also learned the value of being patient for the good of the whole.

❏ Why did you engage in coaching?

As mentioned, during 2003-2005 I had two major strategic issues to overcome: 1) a misaligned sales force that lacked leadership, direction and motivation and 2) a frustrated engineering group who was critical to our success in the new phase of growth. Our existing processes and structure was becoming inefficient, resulting in poor planning, a lack of accountability and a loss of customer focus. We were also getting ready to embark on using new technologies in our products that were driven by our client requests.

The first issue was solved using my own instinct with some help from a sales consultant. During a six-month period I saw people challenging and questioning my leadership. We had a burning platform, no sales and our production capacity was down to half. The times called for drastic measures which we took on and eventually turned the company around. However, as I approached this phase of our development, I was hoping that there had to be an easier way to lead change. I naively signed on to the coaching course to learn how to coach one of my key employees who was needed to make this change happen.

❏ How did coaching help you in your role as President of Proceco?

As you can imagine, prior to coaching I was known as a hands-on, task-oriented, no-nonsense leader. I was having a bit of a crises of confidence and was about to embark on a journey of leading through unchartered territory. I had no compass or tools that I knew of at that time. I later learned to trust myself, draw on my previous successful experiences and leverage my lessons learned. I also was better able to access the right supports to help me through this part of the journey. Previously, I acted independently and did things my way. Coaching helped me to learn while doing. The CEO had confidence in me but I wanted to make sure I was doing everything within my power to position us for success.

Coaching helped me to reflect on my baggage and unclutter my thoughts so that I could act more purposefully and intentionally. I am passionate about my work. I have high expectations and am accountable. I always honor my commitments. My hot buttons are lit up when I work with people who are detached, show no passion, demonstrate a lack of faith and sabotage teamwork. Coaching helped me to focus on my *Use-of-Self* as I led through this journey. I learned how to spot my hot buttons and step back and develop other approaches that showed better results. My thoughts and actions were aligned. Beverley provided me with specific readings, benchmarks, best practices, assessment tools and processes that helped me. She also helped me develop an action plan that I could commit to. I also learned to seek out feedback regularly from my team, Beverley and others to determine if I was being effective in achieving my intentions.

With coaching I was able to better understand my choices and options before taking action. My behavior became more intentional and resulted in more effective results that rippled throughout the organization. I learned about how my actions affected teams, and the company at large. I was able to more clearly articulate the vision. I created senior management buy-in and set objectives and alignment throughout the organization. My leadership style was more humane and respected by others. I built in reflection time, mostly on weekends, to evaluate my progress and strategize for the upcoming week. I now seek feedback and advice when I am fumbling. I also made it transparent to my management team that I was working on changing my Self to more effectively lead the company. This helped me to gain credibility and trust with my employees.

❏ **You moved your company fast and deep. How did coaching help?**

Once I was able to effectively communicate the vision and create a sense of urgency by showing the team why we needed to act, it became easier to set challenging objectives. I struggled with this choice but feel that it was the right thing to do. I rolled-up my sleeves and helped out so that the team could see my commitment. This kept me and the team focused. I listened, heard and acted, which dispelled myths and squashed any rumor mills. The management team was also empowered to do the same and they did so by showing their commitment through action. Beverley was onsite two days a week to provide support to other managers, and we developed a People & Leadership Development strategy to support the changes. This, I believe, demonstrated our investment in our people. I am very proud to say that, at this point in our process, everyone is committed and actively implementing changes within their own span of control.

❏ **What conditions existed to make coaching work for you? Your team? Proceco?**

Synchronicity played a key role in getting us started. I knew intuitively that I needed help but I did not know exactly what this help should look like. I was looking for quite some time for a coach that could fit with our culture. He or she needed to understand the French and

English cultures, as well as the local and international manufacturing business challenges that impact our company. Triple Impact Coaching took into consideration the organizational context. I also had full support from my CEO to embark on this process. We included him in the selection process and check point meetings.

We provided coaching to the management team onsite two days per week, as well as by phone and e-mail between sessions. We really wanted to develop a learning culture which meant spreading this approach throughout the organization. We used the initiatives and business challenges that we faced on a daily basis as a means of examining our assumptions, beliefs, choices and actions. We also developed a leadership profile and competency model which helped us reinforce how we wanted to change. These tools and processes are now strengthening our leadership culture and positioning us for sustainability in the long term.

❑ **What advice would you give to a coach or leader who wants to do Triple Impact Coaching?**

First, you need Senior Management buy-in. This type of coaching does not work if it is not incorporated in the context of your work. The coach needs to build the relationship with your coachee. Trust is crucial. The coach must be accessible and know the business issues. This will help you to gain credibility with your clients who will then be open to trying something new. In my case, this approach was off the beaten track; however, once I understood the process I had full trust in Beverley.

As a leader you need to remember that change takes time. You will need to be fully committed and practice patience, which is not my strong suit, but I am learning.

❏ How do you, as a leader, coach employees to feel motivated and empowered?

Empowerment can be difficult for some people to understand and accept. Too many managers think empowerment means delegation. They understand the definitions but fail to coach others to perform in a manner that ensures the direction, desired outcomes and measures of success are clear. Without this how are employees to know if they are performing and on the right track? Employees also need to have the right skills, tools and coaching to succeed.

What worked particularly well for me was the constant feedback I was getting, which helped me to regain my confidence, dispel myths and old beliefs that I had about myself and others. Reflection continues to help me learn how I empower others and how I disempower them too. I have been soliciting ideas from the team, guiding them in the right direction through coaching and feedback, and letting them go. This is different from the past where I regularly jumped in and did the work. However, I still believe that accountability cannot be transferred until people have proven their ability to successfully complete assignments, so I feel that I still need to provide coaching and feedback. Once they are able to successfully accomplish their objectives, I let them run with it, follow up with feedback to keep them on track and then recognize them for a job well done.

Case Study # 2: VIA Rail - The Power of the Team

Organization Profile

VIA is a passenger rail transportation company operating independently as a Crown Corporation since 1978. With a head office in Montreal, Quebec, VIA services Canada from the Atlantic to Pacific Oceans and from the Great Lakes to Hudson Bay. It has a workforce of more than 3,000 and serves a client base of 3.9 million passengers per year. VIA employees are loyal, dedicated and have a strong sense of pride. Many employees have long standing service. VIA has a strong traditional culture and tight network of employees who share and embrace the vision to be "The Canadian leader of service excellence in passenger transportation."

Coaching Project Context

At the time of this coaching project, VIA was undergoing some major organizational changes. The company was in the midst of making changes at the top. It was without a Chairman of the Board and had an interim President and CEO who had worked for the company for more than 25 years. The newly-hired Vice President of Human Resources was developing the People Strategy that involved a variety of leadership development initiatives that would help the company make the changes required to achieve its vision.

VIA had also gone through a few rounds of downsizing that left some employees with a sense of disempowerment, lack of motivation, innovation and creativity. The organizational structure was traditional and hierarchical and was missing opportunities to fulfill its potential to be more efficient and effective. While they waited for decisions to be made about the Leadership Team, employees and managers felt a sense of urgency. They had operations and a business to run.

Some key initiatives were already underway. Managers had developed a strategic direction and key priorities. They implemented cross functional teams to help break silos and create a flatter, more empowering structure that would help employees provide better customer service.

VIA also provided leadership development for their executive and middle management levels through McGill University's International Masters Program in Practicing Management (IMPM) and the Advanced Leadership Program (ALP). Triple Impact Coaching was offered to the participants in the ALP program as a support to their learning and as a process to help them learn about themselves while working as a team on a company challenge.

The Advanced Leadership Team (ALP) comprises six middle managers (five men and one woman) who represented almost every function of the organization. They began their journey as a group of colleagues, not a formal team. Eventually they would become the ALP Team, a cross functional team working together to examine the customer focus challenge at VIA.

In a little more than nine months, the ALP Team learned how to lead change, create readiness, support and ownership of the customer focus challenge at all levels of the organization. Together they learned how to work as a cross functional team and to leverage their individual contributions to move their challenge forward. In order to make this happen, they aligned their challenge with the Executive direction that included a multiple of customer focus initiatives on organizational, strategic and tactical levels. The ALP Team was instrumental in facilitating the positive outcomes by developing and facilitating a process that led to a two-day retreat that re-energized the organization, created a shift in mindset, and aligned people from across Canada around a common goal and action plan geared to sustainable change.

Three years later, the company is restructured to support a customer focus strategy, with the customer being discussed at every level of the organization. The ALP team continues to meet regularly and has become the think tank for customer focus initiatives at VIA.

Here is a snapshot of the ALP Team's challenges, approach and results.

VIA Rail Canada

Challenge:
- Changes in Canadian transportation and travel market, new technologies, new competitors impacting customer expectations
- VIA needed to adapt to changing environment in order to achieve its vision of being the Canadian Leader in service excellence in passenger transportation
- Wanted to enhance effectiveness of cross functional teams

Approach:
- Cross functional team attended McGill's Advanced Leadership Program & worked on customer focus
- Friendly Consultants Feedback
- Participated in Triple Impact Coaching Program to help them reflect, understand and integrate their learning
- Ensured linkage with other initiatives and transferred their insights and lessons learned to organization

Results:

Shared vision customer focus
- November meeting Operations Planning Committee (OPC) and 4 regional service teams participated in 2 day discussion session
- Objectives were to examine how the organization supported cross functionality and examine how to re-energize the company with a clear focus on the customer
- Created synergy, alignment and commitment to the vision, mission, goals, cross functional culture at all levels

HR People Strategy
- Aligned to support culture changes, leadership development

New Structure for stronger customer focus
- Energized and innovative workforce

The following is a summary of interviews with the ALP Team about their reflections of their coaching experience and advice they have for others considering Triple Impact Coaching for themselves or their organizations.

ALP Team Coaching Program

The purpose of coaching was to help the ALP Team learn about themselves while they were working on the task at hand: Examining customer focus within VIA. The following chart is an overview of the activities that shaped the ALP Coaching Program.

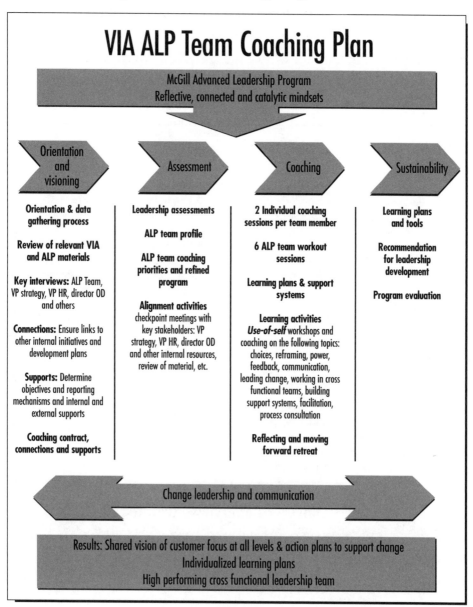

VIA ALP Team Coaching Plan

McGill Advanced Leadership Program
Reflective, connected and catalytic mindsets

Orientation and visioning	Assessment	Coaching	Sustainability
Orientation & data gathering process	**Leadership assessments**	**2 Individual coaching sessions per team member**	**Learning plans and tools**
Review of relevant VIA and ALP materials	**ALP team profile**	**6 ALP team workout sessions**	**Recommendation for leadership development**
Key interviews: ALP Team, VP strategy, VP HR, director OD and others	**ALP team coaching priorities and refined program**	**Learning plans & support systems**	**Program evaluation**
Connections: Ensure links to other internal initiatives and development plans	**Alignment activities** checkpoint meetings with key stakeholders: VP strategy, VP HR, director OD and other internal resources, review of material, etc.	**Learning activities** *Use-of-self* workshops and coaching on the following topics: choices, reframing, power, feedback, communication, leading change, working in cross functional teams, building support systems, facilitation, process consultation	
Supports: Determine objectives and reporting mechanisms and internal and external supports			
Coaching contract, connections and supports		**Reflecting and moving forward retreat**	

Change leadership and communication

Results: Shared vision of customer focus at all levels & action plans to support change
Individualized learning plans
High performing cross functional leadership team

Context:

❏ **Why was coaching important to you? Why did you want an external coach?**

Our discussions, exercises and reflections during our ALP sessions at McGill made us realize that we all were a product of our organization's culture and we shared a common mindset. If we truly wanted to benefit from our investment in ALP, and effect change, we needed an outside perspective, someone not from the same mold, to help us look at challenges in a fresh way. Internal resources were too close, too likely to echo opinions we already shared. We thought they were also part of the problem. We were stuck and wanted help. We couldn't see the forest for the trees.

We needed an unbiased coach, someone who could challenge us and help us challenge one another. We wanted a coach to ask questions, to help us think differently and also ask us the questions that we were unable or unwilling to ask ourselves. We hoped that an external coach would bring new approaches and keep us focused.

Coaching was important. It helped bring our learning to a higher level by using the "tricks" and experience of a coach.

One team member describes why he wanted coaching as follows: "I believe that coaching has an invaluable impact on an organization that has many long service employees. New ideas come from new people. When that does not occur naturally in an organization, then an external coach can help to bring a new perspective to reframe our challenges. A coach will also be able to identify unproductive behaviors that the person or their colleagues are just so used to that they don't realize the impact of those behaviors."

❏ What did you do to establish Triple Impact Coaching at VIA?

Select the right coach for the job

We as an ALP team interviewed our coach. We knew we were about to embark on a major learning process and wanted to have the right relationship with our coach and each other. Chemistry was important.

What makes a good coach?

He or she must be a good listener, have a sense of humor, have the background, skills, credibility, experience, and empathy. The person must be adaptable to the culture of the organization and provide feasible solutions that respect the company culture, yet still help us to grow and develop. Effective coaches must also be flexible and capable of changing their approach and methodology if it is not working.

Integrate your coach into your organization

Integration and exposure is necessary for coaching to be successful. Coaching on its own is good but not enough. One ALP Team member said: "The successful consultants I have worked with, invested in and took time to get to know the company. They learned about why we care enough to do what we are doing on a daily basis. They understand the risk and history of the organization and provide practical and feasible solutions. It's not about how good coaching is but it's the practical, feasible solutions that will make an impact on the team and challenge."

The coach is not a permanent member of the organization. To help her get a touch and feel of the company, we made arrangements for

Beverley to get to know the CEO, VP Strategy, VP HR, Director OD and other people we considered critical for the success of our work, individuals who would play a key role in helping us link our challenge to other initiatives and strategies. We wanted her to experience the environment we were working in, spend time onsite and see the culture in action. We gave her access to talk to people we work with and report to so that she could gain insight into our life at VIA.

This helped us work more effectively as partners in our learning and set the groundwork for the organization to embrace change, and for the team to be supported and ready for change. The critical first step must be establishing the "winning conditions" so that the benefits are obvious for all to see. Once this was in place, we established the right feedback loops to the Executives, other key stakeholders and within the team.

Outside of our courses at McGill and our coaching sessions, our team met regularly to continue our work, challenge ourselves to keep our learning alive, and apply the new concepts that we were learning.

❏ What were the outcomes / results for you in the coaching program? What were your greatest accomplishments, insights or *Use-of-Self* defining moments?

Results and outcomes can be categorized into four themes: teamwork, leadership, personal development and coaching.

Teamwork

Teamwork is a strong value and an essential part of our culture at VIA.

We began as a group, a collection of colleagues who became a team. Some of us worked together in other projects but we had never before worked together as a team. At first, we didn't all get along. We had our biases, stereotypes of each other and one another's functions, many of which were unfair. We were also looking outward, and eventually we realized we needed to look inward, outward and around.

The first task we had as a team was to select the company challenge that we were going to work on in the ALP Program. Selecting this challenge was not easy given our organizational context at that time. Customer focus was something that we were all passionate about and that we thought we could manage within our span of control, making a difference despite possible changes in leadership or direction.

Once we agreed on our company challenge, we quickly learned that we needed to get buy-in from our senior management team. This is where we began our change leadership journey.

As we progressed through our work on our company challenge, we came up against differences in perspective, experiences, ideas and opinions about how to proceed. We fell right into old patterns of behavior that mirrored some of our other organizational challenges. We discovered that we were a microcosm of our own culture and organization. Coaching, experiential exercises, assessments and reflections helped us to see beyond our usual approaches and challenge the limits of what we could do.

One team member recalls a specific time where they as a team were stuck in their old patterns and found a way out. "At McGill we did an exercise where we built a collage that represented our challenge. While working on this exercise we were so determined to resolve the problem quickly and with harmony, that we did not take time to fully respect and discuss various perspectives. We went from A to Z in record time. This is not an uncommon behavior for us. We go from identifying a problem to bringing a solution without taking time to fully understand its cause and, thereby, considering other options."

"Another time this happened was during the planning phase of our 2 day meeting. This behavior frequently repeated itself but most of the time we were able to recognize it and, with the help of our coach, take time to reflect and consider other ways of achieving our objective."

We learned to appreciate other people's approaches to problems and their different perspectives. This opened us to understanding our challenge from different perspectives. We learned to continue working as a team during heated, tense discussions and interactions by being contained, not taking over and damaging the team.

One team member tells of an experience where the team was under a lot of pressure, and stayed contained and respectful until they completed the task. "I remember in one of our coaching work out sessions we did an exercise where we had to work as a team blindfolded to make a perfect square. All of our team members are leaders, yet when we did the exercise we all contributed in different ways and let each other lead at different moments. This behavior allowed us to form a perfect square in a short period of time. A feeling of mutual trust was felt by everyone. There was no resistance to others' suggestions. We were a very cohesive team. We tried to replicate this as we worked together on our challenge."

By knowing the impact that our own individual behavior had on the team, we became more conscious of our choices and actions. We learned to let expertise lead and to be open to being led. We learned about the real power of the team.

It was very exciting to see how we as a group leveraged individual strengths and weaknesses and the positive impact this had on the team's dynamic and performance. "We shared a common mission around a high profile company challenge. We worked closely together on a topic near and dear to our hearts. The expectations and stakes were high. Failure was not an option. We were always on and counted on each other to make things happen," said one team member.

A participant described his learning as follows: "One revelation that I had from this experience is that I am amazed at the impact that a group or individual can have on an organization. Our small team of six people, not Executive VP's, can have an impact and bring about significant high profile change, not skunk work."

Leadership: Leading and Influencing Others

Working on the customer focus challenge provided us with a great opportunity to learn to lead change. We had to wrestle with the challenge, but we were all passionate and believed it was the right thing to do and that it was good for the company. Through our McGill ALP program, we had the opportunity of having a group of friendly consultants (peers) visit and experience a day in the life of VIA. They interviewed people from all parts of the organization and gave us a report on their observations and recommendations. This feedback was not very positive, but it was helpful. We now had a new challenge on our hands — how to share this information so that it is constructive and builds on our sense of pride and duty to our customers. We, as the ALP team, decided that we needed to present the results to the Executive Team. We spent time preparing for our meeting with some of the members of that Executive team. We reframed our challenge from re-energizing the customer, customer experience to customer focus. Many times throughout the process we were confused but we quickly learned that if we were confused, others will be, too. One team member captured the essence of this tension as follows: "Reframing the question and reframing the approach before a group session is the key to achieving the desired results. Unless I challenge the question and approach until they are clear to me, I can not buy-in so why would I expect others to buy-in?"

We spent a lot of time getting our heads around what we wanted to do, being clear about our objectives, communications. We became more structured in our approach. We built agendas to keep our meetings focused. While we were working together, we also got coaching on our team process and tips on how to stay focused and productive. Balancing reflections, emotions, tasks, and learning all at the same time was difficult but essential.

In one of our coaching workout sessions, we brought in our internal organizational development director who was instrumental in helping us develop the right approach to framing our challenge for the Executive Team. He helped us to see ourselves in action and we were quickly able to get unstuck.

We got coaching on our approach and were able look at the task as a learning opportunity and a challenge. We linked our challenge with the CEO's strategy and met with him and the Executive Team. They had the same initial reaction as we did. They were not pleased and said "What do you mean we aren't customer focused?" Our CEO worked with the Company for more than 25 years and had a very good understanding of the challenge, so we came prepared to address the challenges and have a discussion. We helped him and the Senior Management Team reframe the challenge just as we had. He then became the champion for customer focus and the members of the Senior Management Team gave their full support.

This was a turning point. Our initial request was to have a meeting to discuss the customer focus challenge with others in the organization. Our idea got traction and grew into a two-day meeting with the senior management team and the customer service teams from across Canada. We quickly established ways to keep senior management in the loop while we worked on our challenge. We met regularly with our managers who were all on the senior management team to keep them abreast of our thinking.

We then went through a process to help us articulate our objectives and expected outcomes. We realized that we knew what we wanted but we did not know how to get there. We were not process consultants, we had never designed and facilitated a two-day meeting of this kind. We sought help from our coach. She gave us advice and helped us develop our approach, but it was our project. We were accountable and we delivered. We put together our presentations which were reviewed by our coach, the director OD and each other. By the time we presented to the Senior Management Team we were all aligned. We knew who was to play which positions and how they were to play them. We learned how to communicate our ideas, convince others and package information so that people could engage and participate.

The two-day meeting was a huge success. We wanted to update people on what we were learning about customer focus at VIA and explore how we might improve in this area. We did not want to create a new team or be in charge of the customer focus challenge, because we believed this impacted every level and role in the organization. The results exceeded our objectives. More than 60 service team representatives from across Canada and all of the Senior Management Team, including the CEO, participated in the meeting. By the end of our session we had outsourced our challenge. Everyone in the room bought into the customer focus challenge and identified a plan to support the concept. This event re-energized our organization. We lit the spark that would fuel momentum and action for change.

Three years later we have sustainable change. There are many new customer focus initiatives underway. The President is now a strong and vocal advocate of the customer. The organization is aligned and structured around the customer. The ALP Team is a think tank for reviewing customer focus challenges and initiatives. A second ALP team is working on the customer experience. Our Public Affairs department recently held their strategic alignment meeting at one of the maintenance centers so that they could better understand their internal customers and how they impact the customer experience. As part of their two day meeting, the Public Affairs team did job shadowing with the maintenance center staff so that they each could better understand their roles in supporting each other and the customer. The meeting was held in a VIA train so they could also better understand the touch and feel of the train and the customer experience. Today the Customer is mentioned and talked about every day at every level of the company.

Personal Development

Part of the coaching program was focused on their individual learning. Here are some reflections that highlight the challenges and insights from the team members.

"Learning about myself while working on our challenge helped me acquire the skills of successful leadership: I learned to stop, slow down, reflect and observe myself in action. My old habit was to move quickly to respond without looking around. Now, it is my reflex to slow down and be more strategic when I plan and problem solve. I look for ways to collaborate with others and obtain their input and feedback. I think about the connections and the impact my decisions and actions may have on others. I am better able to identify critical challenges and take into consideration the individual, team, group, outside group and other perspectives."

"The fundamental realization that I had was to make the time to reflect and think before reacting. I try to be less sarcastic and more patient in meetings. I am working on my listening skills and trying to avoid finishing other people's sentences."

"It is still fresh in my mind, as if it were only yesterday. I can remember how we acted, interacted and sat during some of our exercises and meetings. I recall how we helped or hindered the team process. Remembering these examples helps me to make more conscious choices about how I want to be in my present work or team situation."

"Feedback in my career has always focused on developing my technical abilities, not my leadership competencies. Through the coaching process I was able to get feedback that was helpful, relevant and timely. Coaching gave me the tools and process to reflect on my leadership profile, strengths and weaknesses. In addition to the one-on-one sessions, watching myself in action through the team workout sessions also helped me learn what I should focus on and set priorities that would help me immediately in my job. I became more conscious about what I do and the impact I have on the team and the challenge.

I learned what I needed to do to move forward. These experiences helped me to reflect and refresh my thinking and approach. I have tools and a process to keep my learning and objectives at top of mind to enable me to make conscious intentions. I believe that personal change happens by knowing my self. I control change."

Coaching Others

The challenge is passing on the concept of continuous learning to our colleagues and using the experiences gleaned in our day-to-day activities. Triple Impact Coaching also helped us to learn how to coach others.

Here are a few reflections on the team's experience coaching others.

"Coaching was the start for me on a personal level to be more knowledgeable about myself, the people I work with and give feedback to. The coaching program brought fresh ideas that helped me in the here and now to understand and deal with real challenges with my teammates as we worked together. Because this was so real, I am now able to pull up these experiences and use my learning to influence current situations."

"I continue to use personal reflections and have started to share the material that I learned with my work team."

"I am now coaching my employees and grooming someone in my group on how to manage the human element of his work. He is technically very sound, but he needs support to set objectives and incorporate more people in his decision making processes. I am coaching him on how to leverage the strengths of his team."

"Coaching helped me to recognize people's strengths, build and leverage different styles and preferences to lead, manage and work effectively in a team. I am much more aware of people's sensitivities. I am also better able to deal with people's feelings and coach others to do the same."

"I realized that change from the "normal" mindset in an organizational setting is very difficult. We quickly fell into our old patterns. Coaching helped me become more aware of my personal role as a coach in my work team. I hold back from acting and reflect on the approach first. ALP Team reflections and coaching helped the team focus and explore different approaches."

Our Advice for others

"The financial situation at VIA Rail and management philosophy has created the use of cross-functional teams both at the service level and for major activities between functions. The concept of coaches is relevant at all levels in the organization from a train crew to the Executive Management Committee. Any benefits from increasing the skill level of coaching will increase the effectiveness of the various teams themselves."

"I believe we had the right team and would have been successful working on our project. However, given the complexities of our organization, without coaching we would not have had the deep impact we experienced on the team, personal and organizational levels, in such a short time. Fourteen cross functional teams exist in the company and the intervention/meeting helped to bring the team tighter together. More got done quicker with deeper impact aligning functions and priorities."

"For coaches who want to work in a team/organizational context like ours, we recommend conducting a half day session for Executives to understand and sell the concept throughout the organization. The framework should be layered on top of the organizational frameworks to support the people initiatives within their own company. At VIA, we leveraged our VP HR and VP Strategy, Director of Organizational Development and the Human Resource Learning Resource to ensure our approach was aligned with their frameworks and People Strategy."

Coaching

Beverley's Coaching Tips

❑ **Build partnerships and align your program with the relevant internal and external resources that are critical to your team's success.**

I worked with the ALP Team at McGill in the ALP Program as one of their instructors and was their coach during the out-of-class sessions. This helped me gain insight and keep abreast of the concepts, terminology and language that influenced their work on the customer focus challenge so that I could integrate the learning in their program.

I also worked closely with the VP Human Resources and Director OD to ensure the coaching program was aligned with their People Strategy. VIA was very generous with their time and availability to provide me with access to the people, resources and materials that I needed to develop the coaching program and related interventions. These partnerships permitted us to leverage existing tools, processes, and other supports quickly and efficiently throughout the program.

❏ Integrate yourself with the organization

The coaching relationship in this type of context is very unique: as you become part of the organization for a temporary period of time, yet have to maintain a degree of distance as an outsider in order to remain objective and effective in your work. There is a degree of risk that is shared by both the coach and the organization. For these reasons, I believe that it is critical to get to know the organization by spending time there. This helps me to understand the culture and decision making processes. It also gives my clients and their supporters an opportunity to get to know me better, and builds trust and credibility.

❏ Know your role and play it well

Always remember that you are there to coach the team members to perform and achieve their objectives. As a coach in Triple Impact Coaching, I played the role of coach, advisor, connector, integrator and facilitator. Know your limits and respect your boundaries.

❏ Don't overload

I like to provide the buffet of experiences and resources which can be overwhelming at times. The challenge is finding the right balance. Leaders, myself included, are high achievers. They are like sponges, they always want more and more. However, as a coach, I have to be careful to provide the right balance of content, process, timing and relevancy so the team can absorb the learning while managing their work, individual and team learning processes and personal life.

❑ Transfer learning and move to action

Sustainable change that moves this fast and deep only happens when there is an organizational readiness to change, alignment and action. You must integrate and connect your coaching programs to the real business and larger learning communities or initiatives that are relevant to your team and organization. Coaching helped the team to make these connections so that they could integrate their learning and move to action faster. This type of teamwork requires partnerships, the ability to take calculated risks, openness, honesty and respect for each other to produce the ripple effect throughout the organization.

For most growing organizations, there comes a point in time when the Human Resources (HR) function must transition from transactional fire fighters to proactive business partners. While this type of transition is a common one, it is nonetheless difficult. Henry David Thoreau once said, "things do not change; we change." The challenge for organizations lie in supporting transformation at the individual level so that it becomes evident at the organizational level. However, many organizations struggle to successfully make this transition. Let's take a closer look at how one organization along with an external coach made it work.

Case Study # 3: Transcontinental Media - HR Transformation

Evolving Towards a Human Resources Business Partner

A Growing Organization

Transcontinental is a printing and publishing business headquartered in Montreal, Quebec, Canada. It is comprised of two printing sectors and one publishing sector (Transcontinental Media). Transcontinental Media is Canada's leading publisher of consumer magazines and the second largest publisher of local and regional newspapers. Its foundation was established in 1979 through the acquisition of one weekly business newspaper and one magazine. A steady stream of acquisitions throughout Canada over the last two decades has made it the fourth largest print media group in Canada with annual sales topping the $500 million mark. Between 1996 and 2003 Transcontinental Media grew from 250 to 2800 employees.

As a result of growth through acquisitions, the organization was made up of a number of independent units throughout Canada. Most acquired businesses retained much of their local policies, infrastructure, cultures and programs. The organization's HR professionals tended to work in silos, were privy to little business information and were focused mainly on local administrative issues related to recruitment, compensation and employee relations in their respective geographic areas. As a result of two major acquisitions in 2000 and 2002, the development of a "one company," HR philosophy became apparent. An internal HR audit, conducted by members of the HR team in early 2003, confirmed the need to better align the HR function and coordinate activities and standardize processes in order to support the organization's growth objectives.

The following chart highlights Transcontinental's challenge, approach and results

Transcontinental Media

Challenge:
- ❏ The Organization had grown too large to maintain a fragmented approach to HR.
- ❏ HR needed a framework to relay the vision and specify the changes required

Approach:
- ❏ Develop a Change Strategy using a collaborative change process
- ❏ Align HR's internal partnerships
- ❏ Involve all three levels in the six phase development process

Results:

Shared Vision of the Future
- ❏ Linked HR as a business partner to strategic priorities
- ❏ Had senior leaders champion & reinforce the vision
- ❏ Built a collaborative HR operating plan

Renewed Patience & Optimism
- ❏ Leadership demonstrated commitment to making visible signs of change e.g. celebrated and recognized quick wins, provided recognition

Collaborative Planning & Transparency
- ❏ Process created a partnership strongly rooted in a culture that values cooperation

Client Focus
- ❏ Strong understanding of the cultural, business, technical and individual context

Non-Dependence
- ❏ Internal ownership of change process by the organizational system, rather than by external resources

For Katya Laviolette, who was hired in May 2003 as Vice-President, Human Resources at Transcontinental Media, two things became apparent in her first months of leadership. First, the organization had grown too large to maintain a fragmented approach to HR. In order to continue growing, acquiring and successfully integrating, the culture needed to shift from that of a collection of small businesses to a unified publishing company. Second, the future of the business would depend on superior human capital. Transcontinental Media's HR organization would need to become a world class partner to the business in order to attract, develop and support talent. This would mean expanding and growing the responsibilities of the HR professionals from a focus on the technical aspects of HR (recruitment, compensation and employee relations) to include the more strategic aspects of HR (change management, communications, organizational and leadership development).

The HR organization decided to use the following model by David Ulrich as a framework to explain the vision of HR and make explicit the changes required in the role of HR professionals in supporting and achieving the organization's vision and objectives.

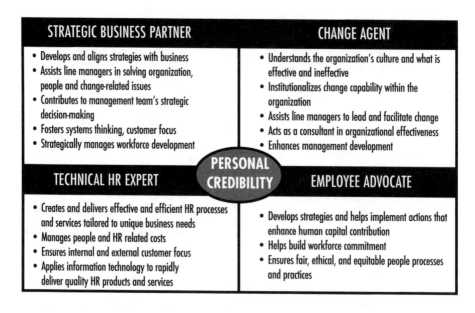

STRATEGIC BUSINESS PARTNER
- Develops and aligns strategies with business
- Assists line managers in solving organization, people and change-related issues
- Contributes to management team's strategic decision-making
- Fosters systems thinking, customer focus
- Strategically manages workforce development

CHANGE AGENT
- Understands the organization's culture and what is effective and ineffective
- Institutionalizes change capability within the organization
- Assists line managers to lead and facilitate change
- Acts as a consultant in organizational effectiveness
- Enhances management development

PERSONAL CREDIBILITY

TECHNICAL HR EXPERT
- Creates and delivers effective and efficient HR processes and services tailored to unique business needs
- Manages people and HR related costs
- Ensures internal and external customer focus
- Applies information technology to rapidly deliver quality HR products and services

EMPLOYEE ADVOCATE
- Develops strategies and helps implement actions that enhance human capital contribution
- Helps build workforce commitment
- Ensures fair, ethical, and equitable people processes and practices

Model for Change

To aid in this transition, Katya Laviolette engaged Beverley to help develop their change strategy. Together, and in conjunction with the HR team, they developed a collaborative change process which built on the current strengths and values of the organization. This model and its transition and implementation process enabled the organization to begin developing competencies that would make it self-sustaining, as opposed to being dependent on external consultancy.

In order to achieve their objectives, each level of the organization that was directly or indirectly impacted by the changes was consulted and/or involved in the change process. For Transcontinental Media this meant that all three levels of organization were active players and participants in various parts of the change process (Corporate, Sector and National HR Team). Collaboration and coaching was the key to the success of this project.

The development process consisted of six basic phases: Understand, Assess, Develop, Test, Implement and Evaluate/Refine. As you will see, this process was used in 2 phases:

Phase 1: Understanding and Strategy Development, and

Phase 2: Execution. Coaching was provided as a support to the team as they worked on their strategy. Each cycle identified and addressed learning opportunities in the areas of the individual, team, structure, culture and organization.

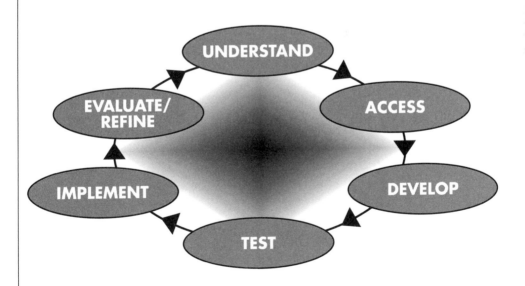

PHASE 1: UNDERSTANDING & STRATEGY DEVELOPMENT

Below is a summary of the activities undertaken and the results achieved in each phase of the cycle during the first rotation.

Understand
- ❑ Completed a review of an HR Audit earlier in the year.
- ❑ Katya Laviolette (VP HR) held individual meetings with the National HR Team, Corporate HR, and local business leaders from every level of the organization to build relationships, understand the business, as well as the HR challenges and objectives, and coached them on the actions moving forward.
- ❑ Beverley Patwell (external coach) held individual meetings with Katya Laviolette, key members of the National HR Team and business leaders to gather data on their strengths, business challenges, cultural dynamics and opportunities for learning and development.

Assess
- ❑ Analyzed data gathered in the "Understand" phase.
- ❑ Identified the HR organization's primary opportunities for development in order to become a more unified team of HR professionals, and expand the role of the HR professional to include competencies in the areas of strategic *Use-of-Self*, thinking and change management. (Ulrich Model).

Develop
- ❑ Articulated vision of the future (Ulrich Model) and gained buy-in with business leaders at both corporate and sector levels.
- ❑ Developed and implemented the first HR National Team meeting with the following results:
    - ❑ Helped the group get to know Katya Laviolette, their new leader;

- ❏ Created a common understanding of business challenges/opportunities driving the need for change;
- ❏ Created a shared vision of the future;
- ❏ Built relational ties across geographical boundaries by involving entire team;
- ❏ Created the first HR Operating Plan linked to business strategy;
- ❏ Conducted deeper understanding of the National Team's leadership styles and preferences; and
- ❏ Identified areas for individual and team learning and development.

Test

- ❏ Reviewed the National HR Team's draft of the joint HR Operating Plan with corporate and business leaders and made appropriate modifications.

Implement

- ❏ Implemented, monitored and evaluated the progress of the HR Operating Plan and corresponding individual action plans were executed over an 8 month period.

Refine & Evaluate

- ❏ Recognized, rewarded and celebrated new behaviors and achievements of operational objectives.
- ❏ Performed periodic reviews of individual action plans and group successes against goals established and identified in the HR Operating Plan.
- ❏ Conducted a post-offsite survey to define and prioritize individual skill development needs for HR team members.

PHASE 2: EXECUTION

One year later a *Use-of-Self* workshop was conducted to help the team move to the next level. Below is a summary of the activities undertaken and the results achieved in each phase of the cycle during the first rotation.

Understand

❑ Reviewed the assessment of the first HR National Team Meeting & the groups' expressed interest in developing their competencies in the areas of coaching, influencing and consulting;

❑ Held individual meetings with functional experts within the HR team, in addition to HR managers, local business leaders and corporate leaders, to understand the impact of the first change cycle as well as their learning opportunities.

Assess

❑ Synthesized data gathered in "Understand Phase" to set priorities for the second HR National Team Meeting to address the following: developing individual strengths and areas for improvement and re-articulated shared vision and operational objectives.

Develop

❑ Developed and implemented a second off-site with the following results:

 ❑ Created fundamental awareness of individual strengths and opportunities for growth particularly in the areas of coaching and influencing skills;

 ❑ Strengthened and displayed individual capabilities by involving HR team members in the design and delivery of the HR National Team meeting;

❑ Built relational ties across geographical boundaries by involving the entire National HR Team; and

❑ Created a second HR Operating Plan linked to business strategy.

❑ Modelled the Triple Impact Coaching process for the team by using it to create and implement the offsite.

Test

❑ Reviewed the National HR Team's draft of the HR Operating Plan with corporate and business leaders and made appropriate modifications;

❑ Obtained feedback from HR Leadership Team and other key stakeholders, as well as internal clients.

Implement

❑ Worked on HR Operating Plan and corresponding individual action and development plans and implemented the actions over a 12 month period.

Refine & Evaluate

❑ Recognized, rewarded and celebrated new behaviors and achievements;

❑ Performed periodic reviews of individual action plans and group successes against goals outlined in HR Operating Plan;

❑ Conducted a post meeting survey that defined and prioritized individual skill development needs for HR team members.

Results/Integration

The process described above has helped the organization establish a shared vision for the role of HR. This vision is owned by HR professionals across the organization, championed by senior management and understood by all business partners. Professionals at the local levels are now more responsible and accountable for the strategic and change management aspects of HR, as well the technical aspects of HR. Furthermore, each HR professional has developed their own learning plan that incorporates the technical, strategic and change management competencies required for their success. The HR competencies have increased across the board. As a function, HR is being called upon to participate in various strategic initiatives. The HR team is now able to set their own performance measures and assess their results. Going forward, the National HR Team has established quarterly meetings to review their progress and work on individual development needs. Finally, a regular annual meeting has been established to structure their HR Operating Plan and focus on continued HR Business Partner training and development.

Conclusion/Keys to Success

For Katya and Beverley, there are a few key lessons they have gleaned from their success in jumpstarting this transformation.

Vision of the Future - On reflection, they both agree that defining a clear vision based on good organizational data was critical. However, it wasn't just having the vision that made the intervention successful. Key success factors included:

❑ linking the HR vision to the strategic priorities of the business and having senior leaders champion and reinforce the vision;

❏ building an HR Operating Plan in collaboration with the National HR Team helped create buy-in and momentum for their work; and

❏ tracking and measuring results on a regular basis reinforced their progress on an individual, team and organizational level and was highly appreciated by every member of the National HR Team.

Patience & Positivism - The bottom line is that no matter how quickly we need to change, change requires patience, a positive vision, and a concrete plan. Leaders must ensure that small but important and visible signs of change are apparent to the organization – especially early on. Key success factors included:

❏ celebrating and recognizing quick wins;

❏ providing recognition (group or individual) for successful interventions and achievements of critical milestones;

❏ identifying and dealing hands-on with varying levels of resistance;

❏ being aware that individuals deal with change in different ways and require varying levels of support; and

❏ taking the time to develop a customized HR approach, as opposed to replicating an approach from previous experience.

Collaborative Planning & Transparency - The change process involved a partnership that was strongly rooted in an organizational culture that valued collaboration. Key success factors included:

❏ including everyone in the design and planning process of the interventions (2 HR National Team meetings, competency development, developing the HR operating plan, developing and monitoring performance measures and individual and team learning/development plans).

Non-Dependence - Beverley's approach to coaching asserts that in order to affect permanent change within an organization, the system cannot become dependent upon the external consultant. Rather, the coach is there to model and provide the process for learning, and in this case some of the content early on. Through this process, the organizational system takes on ownership and becomes responsible for its own learning.

Client Focus - As with any change initiative, it is imperative that the coach begin by developing a strong understanding of the cultural, business, technical and individual context in which she/he will be working. Key success factors in this HR transformation project included:

❑ tailoring the intervention to the culture in order to develop the right strategy to ensure sustained change;

❑ staying constantly attuned to what the client needs by obtaining sound and current data throughout the life of the project; and

❑ being aware of your *Use-of-Self* and monitoring your own strengths and learning opportunities.

CONCLUSION

Our hope and expectation for Triple Impact Coaching is that it will provide some growth opportunities for those of you who are developing your own potential and helping others to develop theirs. While our book was still in the editing stage, Edie was visiting her daughter Kim in California. Kim is teaching college math to math teachers in San Francisco. She was running off a copy of Triple Impact Coaching so that Edie could proofread it one more time. While the printer was running, Kim casually picked up a page of the book and amazingly it turned out to be the Broken Squares exercise. This had been something that Kim had been trying to find for a while so that she could use it to help her math students learn how to make connections with one another, build learning teams that would enhance their work and understand how to build teams in the math classroom to help their students enhance their learning - a Triple Impact for sure.

As Edie explained the exercise and how she uses it in her Triple Impact Coaching sessions, Kim translated how she could use it with her math students and was thrilled to have it - even inviting her mother to come to the session as an observer.

We are hopeful that our experience will be as helpful to you as you read our book and integrate these concepts and exercises in your own coaching contexts.

Enjoy yourselves!

BIBLIOGRAPHY

Broom, Michael (1999) *Power The Infinite Game*. Maryland: Sea Otter Press.

Broom, Michael. (2002) *The Infinite Organization: Celebrating The Positive Use of Power in Organizations.* California: Davies Black.

Brandon, Nathaniel. (1995). *The Six Pillars of Self Esteem*. New York: Bantam Books.

Collins, Jim. (January 2001). *Level 5 Leadership: The Triumph of Humility and Fierce Resolve*. Harvard Business Review.

Collins, James and Jerry Porras. (1994) *Built To Last. Successful Habits of Visionary Companies*. New York: HarperBusiness.

Collins, Jim. (2001) Good to Great: *Why Some Companies Make The Leap and Others Don't*. New York: HarperCollins.

Covey, Stephen. (2004) *The 8th Habit: From Effectiveness to Greatness*. New York: Free Press.

Goleman, Daniel (1997) *Emotional Intelligence: Why It Can Matter More Than IQ*. New York: Bantam.

Heil, Gary and Warren Bennis and Deborah Stephens. (2000) *Douglas McGregor, Revisited: Managing the Human Side of the Enterprise*. New York: John Wiley and Sons.

Jaworski, Joseph. (1996). *Synchronicity of Leadership: The Inner Path of Leadership.* New York: Berrett Koehler.

Kass, Raye. (2005). *Theories of Small Group Development.* 3rd Revised Edition. Montreal Quebec: The Center for Human Relations and Community Studies Concordia University.

Kleiner, Art (1996). *The Age of Heretics. Outlaws and The Forerunners of Corporate Change.* New York: Doubleday.

Luft, Joseph. (1982) *The Johari Window. A Graphic Model of Awareness in Interpersonal Relations.* NTL Reading Book For Human Relations Training.

Maurer, Rick. (2003). *Beyond the Wall of Resistance: Unconventional Strategies that Build Support for Change.* BardPress

Miller, Frederick and Judith Katz. (2002). *The Inclusion Breakthrough. Unleashing the Real Power of Diversity.* San Fransisco: Berrett Koehler.

Mintzberg, Henry. (2004). *Managers Not MBA's. A Hard Look at the Soft Practice of Managing and Management Development.* San Francisco: Berrett Koehler Publishers.

Mintzberg, Henry and Jonathan Gosling (November 2003) *The 5 Minds of a Manager.* Harvard Business Review

Mix, Philip. (September 2006). *A Monumental Legacy. The Unique and Unheralded Contributions of John and Joyce Weir to the Human Development Field.* The Journal of Applied Behavioral Science. A Publication of the NTL Institute. Volume 42 Number 3.

Schein, Edgar. (2004). *Organizational Culture and Leadership.* New York: Jossey Bass.

Seashore, Charles. (1982). *Developing and Using a Personal Support System.* NTL Reading Book for Human Relations Training.

NTL Institute.

Seashore, Charles and Edith Whitfield Seashore and Gerald Weinberg. (1996). *What Did You Say? The Art of Giving and Receiving Feedback*. Maryland: Bingham House Books.

Seashore, Charles N. and Mary Nash Shawver, Greg Thompson and Mary Mattare. (2004) *Doing Good By Knowing Who You Are. The Instrumental Self As An Agent of Change.* The OD Practitioner. Volume 36 Number 3.

Senge, Peter (2006). The Fifth Discipline. *The Art and Practice of The Learning Organization*. New York: Doubleday.

Senge, Peter and Richard Ross, Bryan Smith, Charlotte Roberts, Art Kleiner (1994) *The Fifth Discipline Fieldbook. Strategies and Tools For Building A Learning Organization*. New York: Doubleday.

Senge, Peter and Art Kleiner, Charlotte Roberts, Richard Ross, George Roth and Bryan Smith. (1999). *The Dance of Change. The Challenges to Sustaining Momentum in Learning Organizations*. New York: Doubleday.

Senge, Peter, Otto Scharmer, Joseph Jaworski and Betty Sue Flowers. (2005). *Presence. An Exploration of Profound Change in People, Organizations and Society.* The Society for Organizational Learning. http://www.presence.net

Smallwood, Norm and David Ulrich. (June 2004) *Capitalizing on Capabilities*. Harvard Business Review.

Ulrich, Dave and Norm Smallwood. (2003). *Why the Bottom Line Isn't. How to Build Value Through People and Organization*. New York: Wiley.

There are many people we would like to thank who helped to make this book a reality.

We are both extremely grateful to Dr. Charles N. Seashore, professor at Fielding Graduate University, for sharing his life's work and *Use-of-Self* philosophy with us. We deeply appreciate his unconditional support and mentoring.

We are also grateful to Dale Seguin and Daniel Houle of Mitel, our first Triple Impact Coaching clients. They embraced and championed this coaching approach that began as a course and has developed into a way of working in their organization.

We would like to thank the many organizations who were so generous in promoting our coaching programs and our clients who shared their stories, experiences and research with us. They include the McGill International Executive Institute Desautels Faculty of Management, Niagara Institute, National Training Laboratories, Ottawa Outouais Organizational Development Network, Lewin Center, Concordia University Masters Program in Human Systems Intervention, VIA Rail, Proceco, Transcontinental Media, Ogilvy Renault, Employment and Financial Assistance Branch of the City of Ottawa, Ministry of Public Safety and Security Province of Ontario, La Passerelle and Bombardier.

Special thanks to our proofreaders and graphic designers: Diana Haddad, Kathleen Morrow, Elena Miguens, Charles Raywood, Steve Walters and Celine Maher.

Beverley and Edie would like to acknowledge the people in their lives who supported them throughout their writing journey.

Beverley would like to make the following acknowledgements: I would not have been able to write this book if it weren't for the wonderful coaching and mentoring that I have had in my life. I would like to thank my first mentors, my parents, John and Lucy Patwell. I am grateful for their life long example of the importance of giving back to our families and communities, and for their encouragement and support while I was working on this project. Thank you to three very special high school teachers Joanne Szwec, Barry Mooney and John Maloney who, through their *Use-of-Self*, modeled for me how to coach with spirit, passion and dedication. Special thanks to the memory of the late Bishop Neil Willard who mentored me during my college years and who continues to be an inspiration and influence in my work. Many thanks to my very good friends; Darla Shaw, Glenda Pryce, Lynne Gervais, Wanda Hoskin and Monique Marsan for their encouragement and unwavering support.

I would like to thank my colleagues for their support and contributions to Triple Impact Coaching: Henry Mintzberg, Dora Koop, Jonathan Gosling, Karl Moore, Louise Beauchamp, Jean Lemyre, Karl Coffen, Anthony Rumjahn, Robert Becker, Paul Nadeau Christena Keon Sirsly, Denis Pinsonneault, Paul Cote, Katya Laviolette, Robert Burns, Helmut Schauer, Paula Oke, Kathleen MacDonald, Trevor Anderson and Robert Egery.

Edie's personal acknowledgements are as follows:

I have been very fortunate over many years to have been coached and mentored by many teachers, colleagues, clients, students and family members. A special acknowledgement goes to Charles, my life partner, whose wisdom and humor is evident throughout this book, and to Becky and Kim, my daughters, who are now coaching me as "Moo-Moo," my grandmother role, and to Douglas McGregor who set me up and sent me off on my life-time career in which I have experienced a multitude of coaches and mentors.